Ma~ ~ave
to t me.
The ~ck,
wh~ ~nts
to e~~~~ ~~~~~~~ ~ ~ver
left home.

Macon hates traveling himself. He likes regular routines and a sense of order in the world around him. He would always rather be at home, in his own house – even a house without his son Ethan, who is dead, and his wife Sarah, who has left him.

But things change, things happen . . . Macon goes to stay with his unmarried sister Rose and his two divorced brothers Charles and Porter. His dog Edward starts behaving badly, biting people and chasing them up trees. Muriel the dog trainer from the Meow-Bow Animal Hospital has to be sent for. Then Macon's wife Sarah wants a divorce, and Macon argues with Muriel about training Edward. And Julian, Macon's boss, keeps asking when Macon will finish the next guidebook.

Macon is a kind man, though of~~~
complications. He war
doesn't always know w.
finds out . . .

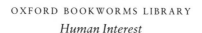

OXFORD BOOKWORMS LIBRARY

Human Interest

The Accidental Tourist

Stage 5 (1800 headwords)

Series Editor: Jennifer Bassett
Founder Editor: Tricia Hedge
Activities Editors: Jennifer Bassett and Christine Lindop

ANNE TYLER

The Accidental Tourist

Retold by
Jennifer Bassett

OXFORD UNIVERSITY PRESS

OXFORD

UNIVERSITY PRESS

Great Clarendon Street, Oxford OX2 6DP

Oxford University Press is a department of the University of Oxford.
It furthers the University's objective of excellence in research, scholarship,
and education by publishing worldwide in

Oxford New York

Auckland Cape Town Dar es Salaam Hong Kong Karachi
Kuala Lumpur Madrid Melbourne Mexico City Nairobi
New Delhi Shanghai Taipei Toronto

With offices in

Argentina Austria Brazil Chile Czech Republic France Greece
Guatemala Hungary Italy Japan Poland Portugal Singapore
South Korea Switzerland Thailand Turkey Ukraine Vietnam

OXFORD and OXFORD ENGLISH are registered trade marks of
Oxford University Press in the UK and in certain other countries

ISBN 978 0 19 479215 8

Printed in China

ACKNOWLEDGEMENTS
Illustrated by: Karen Donnelly

Word count (main text): 24,810 words

For more information on the Oxford Bookworms Library,
visit www.oup.com/bookworms

CONTENTS

PEOPLE IN THIS STORY

Macon Leary
Sarah Leary, *Macon's wife*
Ethan Leary, *their son, dead before the story begins*
Rose Leary, *Macon's younger sister*
Charles Leary ⎫
Porter Leary ⎭ *Macon's older brothers*
Julian Edge, *Macon's boss*

Edward, *the dog*

Muriel Pritchett, *a dog trainer*
Alexander Pritchett, *Muriel's son*
Claire Dugan, *Muriel's sister*
Mr and Mrs Dugan, *Muriel's parents*
Debbie & Dorrie Butler ⎫
Bernice ⎬ *Muriel's friends and neighbors*
Dominick ⎭

1

Breaking up

They were supposed to stay at the beach for a week, but neither of them had the heart for it and they decided to come back early. Macon drove. Sarah sat next to him, leaning her head against the side window.

Macon wore a summer suit, his traveling suit – much more sensible for traveling than jeans, he always said. Sarah wore a beach dress. Her skin was brown from the sun but Macon was still pale. He was a tall, gray-eyed man, with short fair hair, and the kind of skin that easily burns.

Soon the sky grew black and several enormous rain drops hit the roof of the car. Sarah sat up straight.

'Let's hope it doesn't rain,' she said.

'I don't mind a little rain,' Macon said.

A wind blew up and the rain got heavier. Macon pulled out to pass a coach whose wheels were throwing up huge sprays of water from the road, and there was a moment of watery blindness till the coach was left behind.

'I don't know how you can see to drive,' Sarah said.

'Maybe you should put on your glasses.'

'Putting on my glasses would help you to see?'

'Not me; you,' Macon said.

Sarah's hands were holding the edge of her seat very tightly.

'We could stop for a bit,' she said. 'Wait till the rain passes.'

'Sarah, if we were in any danger, I'd have stopped long ago.'

They passed a field where the rain seemed to fall in sheets.

Water ran in rivers across the road, and Sarah had to raise her voice above the noise of the rain on the car roof.

'I don't think you really care that much,' she said. 'The other day I said to you, "Now that Ethan's dead I sometimes wonder if there's any point to life." Do you remember what you said?'

'Well, not exactly,' Macon said.

'You said, "Honey, to tell the truth, it never seemed to me there was much point to begin with." Those were your words.'

'Um . . .'

'You're not a comfort, Macon,' Sarah said.

'Honey, I'm trying to be.'

'You just go on your same old way like before. Your little routines and habits, day after day. No comfort at all. This rain, for example. You know it makes me nervous. What harm would it do to stop a while, show your concern for me?'

Macon stared ahead at the road. 'I drive according to a system, Sarah. You know that. Also, if you don't see any point to life, I can't see why a rainstorm would make you nervous.'

Sarah turned her head away. 'Macon, I want a divorce.'

Macon braked and looked at her. 'What?' he said. He had to look back at the road again. 'What did I say?' he asked.

'I just can't live with you anymore,' Sarah said.

Macon's face seemed thinner and paler. He cleared his throat. 'Honey. Listen. We've had a hard time. People who lose a child often feel this way. Everybody says that a marriage—'

'I'd like to find a place of my own as soon as we get back,' Sarah said. 'You can keep the house. You never did like moving.'

Macon pulled over and stopped the car. He turned off the engine and sat rubbing his knees with his hands. Sarah stared out of the window. The only sound was the drumming of the rain.

✧   ✧   ✧

After his wife left him, Macon had thought the house would seem larger. Instead, he felt more crowded. The windows got smaller, the ceilings lowered, the furniture seemed bigger.

The house itself was very ordinary, standing on a street of similar houses in an older part of Baltimore. The rooms were square and dark, shaded from the hot summer sun by tall trees outside. Their son Ethan's old room was very neat, as tidy and ordered as a room in a Holiday Inn.

Sarah's personal things like clothes were all gone, of course, but it seemed that other things could be personal too. Her sun chair, for example. Macon looked at it, and wondered how an empty space could be so full of a person. He could almost smell her sun oil, and see the reflections in her dark glasses.

Well, you have to carry on. You have to carry on. It was a chance to reorganize, he told himself. You had to have some kind of system to run a house, and Sarah had never understood that. She was the sort of woman who put plates of different sizes in one pile, and who ran the dishwasher with only five forks in it.

He started keeping the kitchen sink full of water at all times. As he finished using each dish, he put it in the sink. Every other day he let the water out, and put in very hot water. Then he put the clean dishes in the dishwasher, using it as a cupboard.

He found a way of doing his laundry that saved water. He took his shower in the evening, and put the day's dirty clothes underfoot, walking up and down on them in the water from the shower. He sewed sheets together to make what he called body bags, which made it quicker and easier to make the bed.

Sometimes he wondered if he was going too far. He imagined Sarah watching him, with a smile in her eyes. He tried to remember the early years, the good times, but it all came back to that last miserable year together, when everything they said was wrong. They were like people running to meet, holding out their arms, but they miss; they pass each other and keep running.

Most of his work was done at home, which was why the house systems were important to him. He wrote guidebooks for people forced to travel on business. Ridiculous, when you thought about it. Macon hated travel. He hurried through foreign countries, with his eyes shut, holding his breath, till he was safely back home, where with a happy sigh he would get on with producing his next passport-sized paperback. *Accidental Tourist in France. Accidental Tourist in Germany. In Belgium.*

He only wrote about cities in these guides, as people taking business trips flew into cities and out again, and their main concern was how to pretend they had never left home. What hotels in Madrid had American-style beds? What restaurants in Tokyo offered American food? Did Amsterdam, Rome, Mexico City have a McDonalds?

Although Macon hated the travel, he loved the writing – the delight of organizing a disorganized country, putting down in short neat paragraphs just the essential information. He spent pleasurable hours over the right choice of words, the correct use of a comma. *I am happy to say*, he would type, frowning in concentration, *that it's possible now to buy Kentucky Fried Chicken in Stockholm.*

❖   ❖   ❖

'But why didn't you tell us?' his sister said on the phone. 'Sarah's been gone three weeks, and I only hear about it today!'

'The last thing I need,' Macon said, 'is my family around me saying, "Oh, poor Macon, how could Sarah do this to you—"'

'Why would I say that?' Rose asked. 'Everybody knows the Leary men are difficult to live with.'

'Oh,' Macon said.

'Where is she?'

'She's got an apartment downtown,' he said. 'And look, there's no need to go asking her to dinner or anything like that.'

'When Charles's wife got her divorce,' Rose said, 'we went on having her to dinner every Christmas, just like always.'

'Yes, I remember,' Macon said wearily. Charles was their oldest brother. 'But she's been remarried quite a while now.'

'Yes. Well,' Rose said. 'Has Sarah been in touch since she left?'

'Once. She came by to pick up a favorite pan, but we didn't talk. I just gave her the pan.'

'We didn't talk. I just gave her the pan,' Macon said.

5

'Oh, Macon. You should have asked her in.'

'I was scared she'd say no,' he said.

There was a silence. 'Well. Anyhow,' Rose said finally.

'But I'm getting along fine!'

'Yes, of course you are,' she told him. Then she said she had something cooking and hung up.

✧　　✧　　✧

Macon didn't eat real meals anymore. When he was hungry, he drank a glass of milk, or ate some ice cream from the fridge. Then he began to notice that his shirt collars felt looser round his neck and the lines on his face seemed deeper. So every morning he cooked two eggs and made fresh, hot coffee. Oh, he was managing fine, just fine. All things considered.

But his nights were terrible.

They began all right. He would get into bed, and move the cat over. The dog, Edward, was small with very short legs, and had to be helped onto the bed. Edward then lay at his feet, while the cat lay next to his back.

Macon would sleep for a hour or two and then wake up. Little worries ran round and round his mind. Had he left the back door unlocked? Forgotten to put the milk away? Paid the gas bill?

The worries changed, grew deeper. He wondered what had gone wrong with his marriage. They were such different people – Sarah changeable and disorganized, he systematic and fixed in his routines. And when Ethan was born, he only brought out more of their differences. Pictures from Ethan's life floated past Macon's eyes like a film on the ceiling. At twelve he'd been a tall, fair-haired boy with an open, friendly face, and a lovable habit of jumping up and down when he was nervous.

Don't think about it.

He was murdered in a burger bar his second night at summer

camp in Virginia. It was one of those deaths that make no sense
– the kind where the gunman has collected his money and is free
to go but decides, instead, to shoot each and every person
through the back of the head.

Blame the burger bar, blame the director of the camp, blame
Sarah for allowing him to leave home, blame Macon for agreeing,
blame Ethan for wanting to go, for not running, for . . .

Don't think about it.

In the end Macon would get out of bed, drink a glass of milk,
and turn on the TV. The cat would sit on his knees, and the dog
usually came and lay on his feet. 'It's just you and me, old
friends,' Macon would tell them.

✧   ✧   ✧

When Sarah phoned, asking if she could have the small rug from
the dining room, Macon agreed. She would come to get it, and
he would invite her in, offer her a glass of wine . . .

'I thought I'd drop over Saturday morning,' Sarah said, 'if
that's convenient.'

But he wouldn't be here then. 'I leave for England tomorrow,'
he said. 'I have to start the new English guidebook.'

'Oh. Well, never mind. I've got a house key; I'll just let myself
in on Saturday.'

'Maybe I could bring the rug over,' Macon said. 'That way
I could see your apartment. I've never been inside.'

'No, it's not fixed up yet.'

'I don't care if it's not fixed up.'

'It's a disaster. Nothing's been done. No curtains, nothing.'

'Nothing? You've been living there over a month.'

'Well, I'm not so wonderfully efficient as you are, Macon.
Some days,' Sarah said, 'I can't even make it out of my bathrobe.'

Macon was silent.

'I wake up in the morning,' she went on, 'and think, "Why bother getting up? Why bother eating? Why bother breathing?"'

'Me too, sweetheart,' Macon said.

'Macon, do you suppose that person has any idea? I want to go and see him in prison, Macon. I want to sit opposite him and I'll say, "Look at me. Look. You didn't kill just the people you shot; you killed other people as well. What you did goes on forever. You didn't just kill my son; you killed me; you killed my husband. Do you understand what you did?" Then when I'm sure he does understand, that he really does realize, I'm going to pull out a gun and shoot him between the eyes.'

'Sarah, it's bad for you to talk like this.'

'Oh? How am I supposed to talk?'

'You'll . . . you'll burn up. It's not productive.'

'Oh, productive! Well, goodness, no, let's not spend our time on anything unproductive.'

Macon rubbed his forehead. 'Sarah, I just feel we can't afford to have these thoughts.'

'Just walk away, Macon. Just pretend it never happened. Go rearrange your tools, why don't you; line them up from biggest to smallest instead of from smallest to biggest; that's always fun.'

'Goddammit, Sarah—'

'Don't you curse at me, Macon Leary!'

They paused.

Sarah said, 'Well, anyhow.'

'So I guess you'll come by while I'm gone,' Macon said.

'If that's all right.'

'Yes, certainly,' he said.

2

Carrying on

For his trip to England, Macon dressed in his most comfortable suit. *One suit is plenty*, he advised in his guidebooks. *It should be a medium gray, which not only hides the dirt but can be worn on any occasion, business or social.*

He packed a small bag and took a last look round, not wanting to leave the safe routines of his house. Then he whistled for the dog and stepped out the front door into the midday heat.

He was taking the dog to the Veterinary Hospital while he was away. Edward did not like staying there, and when they arrived, he began to make little moaning noises and would not get out of the car. Macon had to pull him all the way into the building.

The girl behind the desk asked for Macon's name and gave him a printed form and a pencil. Edward was now standing on his back legs and holding on to Macon's leg.

'Leary. Leary.' The girl pulled a card out of a box, frowning. 'Whoa,' she said. 'Is that Edward? On Rayford Road?'

'That's right.'

'We can't accept him. Says here he bit an attendant. Says, "Bit Barry in the ankle, do not re-admit."'

'What? Nobody told me that when I collected him in June.'

'Well, they should have.'

'Look,' Macon said. 'I'm on my way to the airport, right this minute. I've got a plane to catch.'

But the girl was not interested in Macon's problems, and he went back to the car with Edward. What now? He didn't think

9

his sister would want Edward either, and he certainly wasn't going to ask Sarah for help.

He drove toward home, wondering if he could leave Edward in the house the way he left the cat, with plenty of food and water. Then across the street he saw a sign: MEOW-BOW ANIMAL HOSPITAL. He braked, and made a left turn into the entrance.

Behind the desk in the waiting room stood a thin young woman, with frizzy black hair that came down to her shoulders like a small tent. 'Hi there,' she said to Macon.

Macon said, 'Do you take dogs? I need to leave Edward somewhere for a week.'

She leaned over the desk to look at Edward. Her eyes were very small, like little brown buttons, and her face was sharp and colorless. Edward looked up at her cheerfully.

'You need to have a reservation in the summer,' she said.

'Please,' Macon said. 'I have to catch a plane in an hour, and I don't have anybody to look after him. I'm desperate.'

She seemed surprised. 'Can't you leave him with your wife?'

'If I could do that,' he said, 'why would I be standing here?'

'Oh,' she said. 'You're not married?'

'Well, I am, but she's . . . living somewhere else.'

'Oh.' She came out from behind the desk. She was wearing very short red shorts; her legs were like sticks. 'I'm divorced myself,' she said. 'I know what you're going through.'

'The place I usually take him,' Macon said, 'won't take him again. They say he bit an attendant.'

'Edward? Do you bite?' the woman said. 'How could you do such a thing?' Edward looked up at her happily, and put his ears back, inviting a pat. She bent and stroked his head.

Macon realized he should not have mentioned the biting, but the woman didn't seem to mind.

'So will you keep him?' he asked.

'Oh, I guess,' she said. 'If you're desperate.'

She gave Macon some forms to fill in. 'I'll most likely see you again when you come to pick him up,' she said. 'My name's Muriel. Muriel Pritchett.'

❖   ❖   ❖

'Edward? Do you bite? How could you do such a thing?'

Macon flew to New York, then boarded his flight to London. The woman in the seat next to him looked the talkative type, and Macon quickly took out his book and began reading.

The book was called *Miss MacIntosh, My Darling*, and it was 1,198 pages long. He'd been carrying it around with him for years. He wasn't quite sure what the story was about, but it was always interesting to read a chapter or two.

(Always bring a book, as protection against strangers, advised the Accidental Tourist. *Magazines don't last. Newspapers from home will make you homesick, and newspapers from other places will remind you that you don't belong.)*

When he arrived in London, he went straight to his hotel, changed his clothes, then went out for breakfast. He walked to the Yankee Delight, where he ordered eggs and coffee. The service here was excellent, and the coffee was good, but the eggs were tasteless. He opened his guidebook and made a few notes.

Then he went down the street to the New America, where he ordered more eggs and more coffee. His third stop was a place called the U.S. Open, which had thin and watery coffee.

In the afternoon he visited hotels. He spoke with the managers, tested the beds, checked the bathrooms, tried the showers, and made notes in his book.

By the fourth day he was ready to go home. There was no more to do here, he told himself. He had done everything that he needed to. Well, be honest. At home it was Saturday morning, and Sarah would be collecting the rug. Would she walk round the house, remembering happy times, wishing she still lived there?

He couldn't get an earlier flight, and had to take the flight home he was booked on. Once, Sarah had come to meet him in New York as a surprise. He remembered that meeting so clearly. But this time she didn't even meet him in Baltimore.

He collected his car and drove into the city. Could she be waiting at home? He tried not to let himself hope. He stopped to buy milk and then drove to the Meow-Bow to collect Edward, arriving minutes before closing time.

The woman with frizzy black hair was at the desk. This evening she wore a V-necked black dress with big pink flowers on it, and ridiculously high-heeled shoes.

'Well, hi there!' she said brightly. 'How was your trip?'

'Oh, it was . . . Is Edward all right?'

'Sure, he's all right. He was so good and sweet and friendly!'

'Well, fine,' Macon said. 'Wonderful.' He cleared his throat. 'So could I have him back, please?'

The woman went out the door for a moment, then came back in. 'Caroline will bring him,' she said.

There was a silence. The woman waited, smiling at Macon.

'Um,' Macon said finally. 'Maybe I could pay.'

'Oh, yes. That'll be forty-two dollars,' she said. 'And did I mention before that I train dogs? My speciality is dogs that bite.'

'That must be a dangerous job,' Macon said politely.

'Oh, not for me! I'm not scared of a thing in this world,' the woman said. 'I studied with a man who used to train police dogs. Edward wouldn't bite *me*, of course. He just fell in love with me.'

'I'm glad to hear it,' Macon said.

'But I could train him not to bite other people. You think it over and call me. Muriel, remember? Muriel Pritchett.'

She gave Macon her business card. A girl came in with Edward, who went mad with delight at seeing Macon.

'Well, I'll remember that,' Macon said. 'Thank you.'

'Or just call for no reason! Call and talk.'

'Talk?'

'Sure! Talk about Edward, his problems, talk about anything!

13

Pick up the phone and just talk. Don't you ever feel like doing that?'

'Not really,' Macon said.

Then Edward barked loudly, and the two of them left.

✧ ✧ ✧

Well, of course Sarah wasn't there. He knew it the moment he stepped into the hot, airless house. Really he'd known it all along. He'd just been fooling himself.

The cat ran past him and escaped out the door, and the dog ran round the house, smelling everything and rolling on all the floors. Macon unpacked, took a shower, and did his laundry. The sight of it hanging up over the bathtub reminded him of travel. Where was the real difference? *Accidental Tourist at Home*, he thought, and he climbed wearily into his body bag.

✧ ✧ ✧

When the phone rang, Macon dreamed it was Ethan – Ethan calling from summer camp, wondering why they'd never come to get him. 'But we thought you were dead,' Macon said.

The phone rang again and Macon woke up.

'Macon! Welcome back! How was the trip?'

It was Julian Edge, Macon's boss. He was younger than Macon, and a loud, cheerful man, even early in the morning.

'It was okay.'

'So I guess you start writing up your notes now. When do you think you'll have finished the new book?'

'I don't know,' Macon said.

There was a pause. 'I guess I woke you,' Julian said. 'Anyway, can I expect it by the end of the month?'

'No. I can't do it,' Macon said. 'I'm not organized.'

'August thirty-first, Macon. That's four full weeks away.'

'It's not enough,' Macon said.

'Well. All right, then. Mid-September. How's that?'

'I don't know,' Macon said.

His voice sounded dull and strange, even to himself. After another pause, Julian said, 'Hey, Macon. Are you okay?'

'I'm fine! All I need is time to get organized. You'll have the book by September fifteenth. All right?' Then he hung up.

❖   ❖   ❖

All he needed was time to get organized. Maybe he couldn't get his guidebook organized, so he would organize the house. There was something comforting about that, and over the next week or so he went all through the house, setting up new systems.

He rearranged the kitchen cupboards, and he hung a clothes line across the basement so that he wouldn't have to use the clothes dryer. Dryers used so much electricity. Then he disconnected the wide exhaust tube, and taught the cat to go in and out through the hole in the window where the tube used to be.

He put the clothes basket on little wheels so that he wouldn't have to carry it across the basement, which would save his bad back. Also, thinking of his back, he set up a long tube from the back door down into an automatic feeder box in the basement. Now when he bought Edward's dog food (dogs ate so much food), he could pour it straight down the tube and not have to carry the heavy bags too far from the car.

Unfortunately, Edward seemed to be scared of the basement for some reason, so Macon had to carry him down the basement stairs for every meal. Which was not good for his back.

Sometimes he wondered if all his systems were, well, silly.

The neighbors must have learned by now that Sarah had left him because they started inviting him round for 'family suppers'. One neighbor, Sue Carney, kept leaning across the table to pat his wrist. 'Come and eat with us any time, Macon,' she said.

He thanked her, and moved his wrist away as soon as possible. Sarah had often told him he didn't need other human beings. She was very fond of parties, or had been, until Ethan died.

He and she had met at a party. They'd been seventeen years old, and Sarah had been the bright, sociable one, surrounded by boys, popular with everyone. She had liked Macon, she told him later, because he'd been mysterious and silent, and always wore black (he'd been planning to be a poet at the time).

They married when they both finished college. It was seven years before Ethan was born, and by that time Sarah was no longer calling Macon 'mysterious'.

Didn't she believe he still loved her? Macon wondered if he was cold and unfeeling. But he missed her, he really did, and he did not understand why she had gone away and left him.

✧   ✧   ✧

Some woman phoned and said 'Macon?' It wasn't Sarah; this voice was different. 'It's Muriel. Muriel Pritchett,' she said.

'Ah, yes,' he said, but he had no idea who she was.

'From the vet's,' she said. 'You remember? I was just wondering how Edward was.'

Macon looked at Edward, who was lying flat on his stomach with his legs straight out behind him.

'He looks all right to me,' Macon said.

'I mean, is he biting? He ought to be trained, you know.'

'Well, he's four and a half now—'

'That's not too old! Maybe I could just come around for a drink or something, and we could discuss Edward's problems.'

'Oh . . . I think, um, for now I'll try and manage on my own.'

'Well, I can understand that,' she said. 'I'll wait for you to get in touch, then. You still have my card, don't you?'

Macon said he did, though he didn't know where it was. He

hung up and went back to his guidebook. *Generally food in England is not as bad as some people say it is. Nice cooked vegetables . . .*

❖   ❖   ❖

By September he had only written a few pages of his guidebook, and he began to feel he was falling apart. In the basement the laundry took days to dry on the line, and one morning he decided to re-connect the exhaust tube of the clothes dryer. Better to use a little more electricity than to get depressed over wet laundry.

He put some of the wet clothes into the dryer and turned it on. At the top of the stairs Edward was complaining. He was hungry, but not brave enough to come down the stairs on his own. Macon went up and carried him down.

He was near the bottom of the stairs when a sudden, awful howl rose from . . . where? Edward jumped out of Macon's arms into the remaining wet laundry on the line, which knocked him back against Macon's chest. Macon stepped blindly sideways, put one foot in his wheeled clothes basket, and went crashing to the floor, with his left leg bent double beneath him.

The cat, used to coming in through the hole in the window, had met a hot, wet, whistling wind, but was determinedly trying to climb into the exhaust tube, howling desperately all the time.

'Wouldn't you think,' Macon said to Edward, on the floor next to him, 'that fool cat would know the dryer was running?'

In spite of the pain in his leg, he managed to turn off the dryer and watch the cat escape safely, before beginning the long hard trip up the stairs for help.

3

Back with the family

'*Oh, I've done wrong and I've told lies,*' Macon's sister sang in the kitchen. '*I've been foolish and unwise . . .*'

Macon lay on the daybed in his grandparents' sun porch, and listened to Rose singing as she got the breakfast. She had a high, shaky voice that sounded like an old lady's, though she was the youngest of the four Leary children. She had never left home because there had always been someone she had to take care of. Their grandparents had got old and ill, one after the other, and then it was her brothers. First Charles, the oldest, and then Porter, the next brother, had failed in their marriages and come back home. And now Macon had come as well, to lie there with his broken left leg in plaster and be looked after by Rose.

She was pretty in a quiet, serious kind of way, and ran the house efficiently, being as neat and organized as all the Leary family. Everything in her kitchen cupboards was arranged in perfect alphabetical order – rice, salt, soup (fish), soup (tomato), soup (vegetable), sugar, tea . . .

Charles and Porter managed the business that Grandfather Leary had begun in 1915, a factory making bottle caps. All four of them had spent most of their childhood with their grandparents as their father, Grandfather Leary's only son, had been killed in World War II. For a while they had lived with their mother Alicia in California, but she was a bright, irresponsible young widow, full of wild enthusiasms and sudden changes of life plan. The Leary children rarely shared her enthusiasms, and they were quite happy when she sent them to live with their dull, safe, serious grandparents in Baltimore, while she traveled round the world with her latest husband.

As he sat in front of his typewriter in the dining room, Macon felt strangely at peace with the world. No one else had any idea where he was – not Julian, not Sarah, not anyone. Macon liked that, and had said to Rose, 'I wish things could stay this way.'

'Why can't they?' Rose said. 'We don't need to answer the phone if anyone calls. We'll just let it go on ringing.'

However, that afternoon the doorbell rang and it was Garner Bolt, a neighbor from home, complaining that everyone in the street was worried that Macon had died, seeing all the mail piled up inside the door, not knowing what to think.

'So I brought your mail around to your sister's, to ask if she knew where you were. I promised your friend I'd find out.'

'What friend?' Macon asked.

'Thin little lady with a lot of hair. Saw her standing on your porch, knocking at the door. Pointy high-heeled shoes.'

Macon thought for a moment. 'The dog lady,' he said. 'Jesus.'

Garner finally left, having told Macon how to get back with Sarah and save his marriage. Macon made no reply to any of this advice. He'd noticed lately that he had stopped missing Sarah. He began to wonder what had happened to the twenty years of his marriage, and that evening, as he sat at the table with his sister and brothers, he had a sudden cold shock of fear. Here they all were, playing the same old card game they had played as children. Had anything really changed in thirty years?

✦   ✦   ✦

'Help! Help! Call off your dog!'

Macon stopped typing and listened. He could hear barking and the voice sounded very close. He didn't think it could be Edward because Edward was taking a walk with Porter. But Edward had been behaving strangely for a while, barking and showing his teeth when anyone came to the house, or tried to leave it.

Macon got up, and made his way on his crutches to the porch. Sure enough, it was Edward. He was jumping up and barking madly at the foot of the big tree in the front yard. With some difficulty Macon went down the steps and caught the end of Edward's leash. He looked up into the leafy shadows of the tree.

'Is there someone there? Who is it?' he asked.

'This is your employer, Macon.'

'Julian?'

Julian climbed down the tree. There was dirt on his trousers and his usually neat dark hair was sticking out in all directions. 'Macon,' he said, 'I really hate a man with a horrible dog.'

'Well, I'm sorry. I thought he was off on a walk.'

'By himself?' Julian brushed some leaves off his jacket. 'What happened to your leg? And where's the book? You said you'd finish it in September, and it's now October.'

'It's kind of hard to explain,' Macon said. 'How did you find me, anyway?' He led the way into the house.

'Your neighbor told me where you were.'

'Oh. Garner.'

They went into the living room. Julian chose the most comfortable chair and sat down. 'Where's Sarah?' he asked.

'Who?'

'Your wife, Macon.'

'Oh. Um. She and I are . . .' He found he could not say the word 'separated'. It was something that happened to other people. 'She's got an apartment downtown.'

'You've *separated*?'

Macon nodded.

'Jesus. What went wrong?' Julian asked.

'Nothing!' Macon said, a little too loudly. He lowered his voice. 'I mean, that's not something I can answer.'

The front door banged and Edward ran into the hall, barking noisily. Rose and Charles came in, carrying groceries in brown paper bags, and came into the living room. Macon had to introduce everybody. Julian seemed fascinated.

'Macon Leary with a sister! And a brother too! Who would have guessed it! Macon Leary with a family!'

Rose gave him a polite, puzzled smile, and Macon suggested that she and Charles went to put the groceries away, rather than standing there and holding them. He was afraid that Julian was about to go into his 'Macon Leary' routine. Ever since they had first met, Julian seemed to think Macon was an amusing oddity, someone who was not quite in touch with the modern world.

They had met about twelve years ago, when Macon, wanting to escape from the boredom of the bottle-cap factory, was trying to become a journalist. He wrote a piece for a local newspaper about a trip to Washington, telling readers how foreign the city seemed, and how to make themselves feel they were back home in Baltimore. Julian had called him the next day, with the plan for the *Accidental Tourist* guidebooks – guidebooks for people who would rather be at home in their own living rooms.

Macon went to get the work he had done on the new guide for England. 'It's nearly finished,' he told Julian. 'You can take all this, and I'll send the last chapters as soon as I've finished.'

'Good. After this I want to start on the U.S. again.'

Macon sighed. 'So soon?' He thought wearily of yet more trips to Boston and Atlanta and Chicago . . .

'Things are changing every minute, Macon,' Julian said. 'And who wants to buy an out-of-date guidebook?'

Julian stood up to go, and Macon struggled on to his crutches. Edward, hearing sounds of departure, went mad, barking and running about in the doorway, trying to prevent anybody from leaving. 'Edward, stop it!' Macon shouted over the noise.

They moved toward the front door, and when Edward tried to block it, Macon bent down to pick up the end of the leash and pull Edward away. When Edward felt the leash, he growled fiercely, turned and buried his teeth in Macon's hand.

'Whoa, there!' Julian said. 'Macon? Did he get you?'

Macon looked down at his bleeding hand. 'I'm all right.'

'I wouldn't have a dog like that,' Julian said. 'I'd shoot him.'

Edward was now sitting quietly, looking ashamed. 'Why don't you go now, Julian, while he's calm,' Macon said.

Julian slid through the door sideways, looking back at Edward. 'That is not a well dog,' he said as he disappeared.

Macon tapped his way on his crutches to the kitchen and found Rose and Charles there with Porter, who had now returned from his failed walk with Edward.

'Rose?' Macon said. 'Edward's given me a little sort of bite.'

The three of them turned to look at Macon's hand, which was now hurting him quite a lot. 'Oh, Macon!' Rose cried.

'You need to get that properly cleaned,' Charles told him.

'You need to get rid of that dog,' Porter said.

'It was an accident,' Macon said. 'He didn't mean any harm.'

'Didn't mean any harm? Huh! You should get rid of him.'

'I can't,' Macon said.

'Why not?'

They waited.

'He's not a bad dog at heart,' Macon said. 'Just a bit excitable.' And he'd been Ethan's.

Ethan had brushed him, bathed him, rolled with him on the

floor, played ball with him in the yard. When Edward fell over the ball in his enthusiasm, Ethan's laugh rang out so high and clear, such a joyful sound floating through the summer evening.

'I just can't,' Macon said.

There was a silence.

'He's not a bad dog at heart,' Macon said.

Rose was gently bandaging his hand. 'Maybe he should have some obedience training. How about that woman you told us about, at the Meow-Bow? Why don't you call her?'

'Maybe I will,' Macon said. He wouldn't, of course. The woman had seemed a bit strange to him.

❖   ❖   ❖

On Sunday morning Edward tried to attack a neighbor who'd stopped by to borrow a tool. On Sunday afternoon he threw himself at Porter to stop him leaving the house. Porter had to slip out the back when Edward wasn't watching. On Monday, when Edward went for a walk with Rose, he attacked a passing runner and his leash pulled Rose off her feet.

She came home with a painful knee. 'Have you called the Meow-Bow yet?' she said.

'Not quite,' Macon said.

Rose looked at him in a strange way. Later, Macon realized it was a kind of pity.

❖   ❖   ❖

'Meow-Bow Animal Hospital.'

'This is, ah, Macon Leary. Is Muriel there, please?'

'Oh, Macon! Hi there! How's Edward doing?'

'Well, he's getting worse. He's been attacking people, and growling and biting, chewing things . . .'

Muriel offered to come out five or six times a week to give training lessons at five dollars a lesson. 'That's a special fee for a friend,' she said. 'Mostly I charge ten dollars.'

4

Training Edward

The first lesson was about sitting. Edward met Muriel at the front door with his usual wild barking and jumping, but Muriel more or less walked right through him and pointed at his rump and told him to sit. Edward stared at her. She then bent over and with a long pointed finger pushed his rump down.

'Now you kind of cluck your tongue,' she told Macon, doing it herself to show him. 'That means you're pleased with him. You have to praise them when they do things right. And when I hold my hand out – see? That means he has to stay.'

Edward stayed, but gave a short bark every few seconds. Muriel didn't seem to hear, and began to talk about herself. Macon wondered how long she expected Edward to sit there.

'When I was a little girl, I didn't like dogs at all, can you believe that? All I was interested in was how to change the way my hair looked. My natural hair is real straight and now look at it! I had it done and it made it so frizzy I can't even brush it.'

'Maybe you could just comb it,' Macon suggested.

Muriel shook her head. 'It's hard to pull a comb through it.'

'Shouldn't we let Edward up now?' Macon asked anxiously.

Muriel snapped her fingers over Edward's head. 'Okay!' she said, and Edward jumped up, barking.

Edward learned to sit when Muriel pointed, and then it was Macon's turn. He pointed to Edward's rump. Edward stood fast. Macon frowned, and pointed more fiercely. He felt foolish.

'Push him down,' Muriel said.

Macon leaned one crutch against the wall, and bent stiffly to push Edward's rump with a finger. Edward sat. Macon clucked. Then he straightened and backed away, holding out his hand, but instead of staying, Edward got up and followed him.

'Ssss,' Muriel said, between her teeth. Edward sat down at once. 'He doesn't take you seriously,' she said.

'Well, I know that,' Macon said crossly.

His broken leg was aching, but the lesson went on, and Muriel went on talking and asking questions. She told Macon how lucky he was to get to travel to all kinds of places, like Paris, how wonderful, and write guidebooks about them. She herself had never even been on an airplane, did he realize that?

When she had gone, leaving a new leash with a special training collar for Edward, Macon and Edward practiced for the rest of the day. By suppertime, Edward had learned to sit and stayed there, complaining and rolling his eyes, while Macon clucked in praise. A cluck was now part of the family language. Charles clucked over Rose's baked potatoes. Porter clucked when Macon dealt him a good hand of cards.

During the evening Edward chewed a pencil to pieces, stole a bone from the kitchen, and was sick on the sun porch rug. But now that he could sit on command, everyone felt more hopeful.

❖   ❖   ❖

'When I was in high school,' Muriel said, tapping her foot at Edward, 'my teachers told me I should go to college. But, well, I didn't. That was because of Norman, mostly. My ex-husband. He was just dying to marry me, you see, but we were awful young to get married. I was seventeen. He was eighteen.'

On the second lesson they had done walking to heel, and now in the third lesson Edward was supposed to be learning to lie down and stay. It was not going well. Edward just looked away when Muriel gave the command, which was two taps of the foot. In between telling Macon about her ex-husband Norman, Norman's dog, Norman's mother, and Norman's mother's car, Muriel had to keep pulling Edward's front legs out from under him and forcing him to lie down.

When it was Macon's turn to do this, he had to use the hall table to pull himself back on his feet. 'This is very difficult. I don't suppose *you* ever broke a leg,' he said accusingly.

'I broke an arm once,' Muriel said.

'An arm is no comparison.'

'I did it training dogs, in fact. A big German guard dog. He knocked me off a porch, and then stood over me, showing all his teeth. But only one of you can be boss. So I tell him, "Absolutely not", and hold out my left hand and stare into his eyes.'

'Jesus,' Macon said.

Muriel had lots of stories about her dog-training experiences. 'I've had no failures yet. And Edward's not about to be my first,' she told Macon. 'You keep practicing and I'll be back Saturday.'

All that afternoon Edward refused to lie down. Macon tried everything. Rose and the boys edged around the two of them, politely avoiding any involvement in this private argument.

The next morning Edward attacked the mailman. 'We're not solving the real problem,' Macon told Edward. He tapped his foot twice. Edward did not lie down.

In the afternoon Macon called the Meow-Bow. 'May I speak to Muriel, please?' he asked.

'She's not working today,' a girl said. 'Her little boy is sick.'

He hadn't known she had a little boy. It changed the way he thought of her; she was a different person from the one he'd imagined.

✧   ✧   ✧

Rose was going downtown, and agreed to drop Macon off at Julian's office. He wanted to deliver the rest of his guidebook.

Julian greeted him cheerfully. 'Ah, here he is! *Accidental Tourist on Crutches*,' he said, enjoying his own joke.

They discussed the U.S. guides that Macon would soon be starting work on, and then Macon got up to go. 'My sister's picking me up outside,' he explained.

'Ah yes, the Macon Leary family,' Julian said. 'Why don't I step outside and wait with you. Say hi to your sister.'

Macon suspected Julian of hoping for more Leary oddities to laugh at. Today Rose was wearing an old hat that had been her grandmother's. Macon really didn't want Julian to see that hat.

'Well, I don't think so, really. We need to get home.'

Julian leaned back in his chair. 'Macon,' he said. 'Couldn't you just once invite me to a family dinner?'

Macon avoided answering this directly, and on the way home with Rose he decided that the trouble with Julian was that he had no children. People who had no children, Macon felt, had never truly grown up. They weren't quite . . . real.

Unexpectedly, he thought of Muriel, lying with a broken arm and a German guard dog standing over her, its teeth at her throat. But she didn't give in. 'Absolutely not,' she said.

❖   ❖   ❖

She arrived the next morning in high-heeled black boots and a raincoat. Edward danced around her. She pointed to his rump. He sat, and she bent to pick up his leash.

'Is your little boy better?' Macon asked her.

She looked at him for a moment. 'Who told you he was sick?'

'Someone at the Meow-Bow, when I phoned. Is he okay now?'

'Oh, yes. It was some little stomach thing. How come you phoned?' she asked.

'I wanted to know why Edward wouldn't lie down. I tap my foot but he never obeys me,' Macon said. 'Something's wrong. I've been practicing two days now and—'

'What do you expect? You think I can do magic or something? Why blame me?'

'Oh, I'm not blaming—'

'You most certainly are. You tell me something's wrong, you call me on the phone—'

'I just wanted to—'

'You think it's strange I didn't mention Alexander, don't you? You think I'm some kind of unnatural mother.'

'What? No, wait a minute—'

'You're not going to give me another thought, are you, now you know I've got a kid. Oh no, I won't bother with *her*, you think. And you wonder why I didn't tell you about him before. Well, isn't it obvious? Don't you see what happens when I do?'

Muriel's voice got higher and higher, and Edward began to growl. Macon looked down at him and saw the hair on the back of his neck standing up stiffly. A bad sign.

Muriel looked down too and stopped speaking. She tapped her foot twice, but Edward not only failed to lie down; he rose from his sitting position. Then with a howl he jumped straight at Muriel's face.

At once Muriel raised the leash with both hands and lifted Edward completely off the floor. He hung by his collar, making little noises in his throat.

'He can't breathe,' Macon said. 'Stop it. It's enough!'

Still she let him hang. Macon shook Muriel's shoulder and then Muriel lowered Edward to the floor. He landed in a boneless heap. Macon knelt next to him. 'Oh, God, he's dead!'

Edward raised his head and licked his lips weakly.

'See that?' Muriel said cheerfully. 'When they lick their lips, it's a sign they're giving in.'

Macon stood up. He was shaking. 'Don't you ever, ever do that again. In fact, don't even bother coming again.'

There was a surprised silence.

'Well, fine,' Muriel said. 'You want a dog you can't control? If that's the way you feel, that's fine with me.'

'You want a dog you can't control?' Muriel said.

'I'd rather have a barking dog than a damaged, scared dog.'

'You want a dog that bites all your friends and neighbors? A dog that hates the whole world? A mean, nasty, angry dog?'

She stepped neatly around Edward and opened the front door, then turned back to look into Macon's face.

'Why, yes, I guess you do,' she said.

❖   ❖   ❖

Macon continued practicing with Edward every day, and thought that Edward was slowly getting more obedient. His family was not so hopeful. 'What about when you start traveling again?' Rose asked. 'You're not leaving him with me.'

It was hard for Macon to imagine starting his travels again. Sometimes he wished he could stay in his plaster. In fact, he wished it covered him from head to foot. People would knock on the plaster wall. 'Macon? You in there?' Maybe he was, maybe he wasn't. No one would ever know.

One evening Julian stopped by with some papers for Macon's New York trip. Rose offered him some coffee, which he accepted eagerly, much to Macon's annoyance, who was sure Julian was hoping for some Leary oddities.

'What do you do for a living, Charles?' Julian asked, when they were all sitting down in the living room.

'I make bottle caps.'

'Bottle caps! Is that a fact! And Rose? Do you work?'

'Yes, I do,' Rose said, in her serious way. 'I work at home; I keep house for the boys.'

The telephone rang. Since Macon's return home, the Learys had got into the habit of not answering the phone, but there was a chance this was Porter, who had gone out to buy a hammer and who often got lost, even in his own neighborhood.

They discussed it urgently.

'What do you think?'

'But he knows we wouldn't answer.'

'Yes, he'd surely call a neighbor instead.'

'On the other hand . . .'

It was Julian's fascinated expression that decided Macon. He picked up the receiver. 'Leary,' he said.

It was Sarah. 'I think we should talk,' she said to Macon.

✧   ✧   ✧

They agreed to meet for supper in the Old Bay Restaurant the next evening. Macon wore his gray suit coat and gray trousers with one leg neatly cut off at the top of the plaster. Rose had cut his hair, and Porter had lent him his best tie.

He was the first to arrive, and when Sarah came in, she greeted him in a cool, distant sort of way, like neighbors meeting at a drinks party. They sat down and ordered their food.

'So, why are you living with your family?' Sarah asked.

'Well, because of my leg. I can't manage the steps at home.'

'And what happened to your hand?' she asked.

'Um, Edward bit it,' Macon said. 'He's getting kind of out of control, to tell the truth.' He told her about the trainer he had hired, and how cruel she had been when Edward tried to bite her.

'Ridiculous,' Sarah said. 'He was only frightened; that's why he attacked. There's no point in making him even more scared.'

Macon felt a sudden rush of love.

Oh, he'd had moments when he'd almost hated her, but the fact was, she was his oldest friend. She was part of his life. It was much too late to cut her out.

'What Edward needs,' she was saying, 'is a sense of routine.'

'Sarah,' he said, 'it's been awful living apart. Hasn't it?'

Sarah looked at him. 'I asked you here for a reason, Macon.'

He could tell it was something he didn't want to hear.

'I've been talking to a lawyer about our separation,' she said.

Their food arrived, plates were put down, knives and forks arranged. Macon waved the waitress away.

'I think you ought to come home,' he said. 'Can't we try—'

'I'm trying to make a new life for myself,' she said. 'New directions, different. We didn't have much left, did we? When you broke your leg, who did you call for help? Your sister Rose!'

'If I'd called you, would you have come?'

'Well . . . but you didn't call me. You called your family, and that's where you're happiest, isn't it? The kind of family that always fastens their seat-belts, that has to have a group discussion before they can decide whether to close the curtains. And the best house in the world might be for sale, but you can't buy it because you've ordered a thousand address labels for the old house, and you have to use them up before you move.'

'That wasn't me, it was Charles,' Macon said.

'Charles, you, it's all the same.' Her eyes were full of tears. 'Macon, I know you loved Ethan, but you're not so torn apart by his death as I am. You seem unfeeling, unchanged.'

'Sarah, I'm not unfeeling. I'm . . . just trying to survive.'

'Survive, yes. Survive unchanged by any experience, just like those silly travel books you write. You're empty, dried up, Macon, and nothing really touches you.'

She put her coat on, clumsily. 'So anyway,' she said. 'You'll get a letter from my lawyer.'

Then she stood up and walked out.

5

Limping onward

When the doctor removed the plaster, Macon's leg came out dead-white and ugly. He still limped a bit, but he now had no excuse for not getting on with the new U.S. guides that Julian wanted. The New York trip was the first one, and Rose drove him to the station to catch the train.

She was worried about Edward. 'I wish you weren't leaving him with me,' she said. 'You know how out of control he gets.'

'What could happen in such a short time?' Macon said. 'I'll be home by tomorrow night. If worst comes to worst, you could lock him in the pantry till I get back.'

New York was a foreign city to Macon. He could never get used to the sense of purposefulness there – everyone was always rushing somewhere without a moment to look around them. He began his usual visits to hotels and restaurants, making notes in the old guidebook in his tiny, neat handwriting.

In the evening Julian wanted him to try a new restaurant, which was on the top of an impossibly tall building. The cab-driver who took him there clearly thought it was a bad idea.

'Cup of coffee there will cost you five dollars,' he told Macon.

Most of the people in the restaurant were in evening dress and seemed to be celebrating something. Macon was given a table without a view, and after he had given his order, he took his drink over to one of the great black windows that encircled the room from floor to ceiling.

All of a sudden, he thought he had died.

He saw the city far below him like a shining golden ocean, the streets tiny lines of light, the sky a purple hollow that went on forever. It wasn't the height; it was the distance – his huge, lonely distance from everyone who mattered, Ethan, Sarah . . . He had gone too far, he would never, ever get back.

His heart began to beat twice as fast as normal and his hands shook. He dropped his glass, and ran clumsily across the room and out the door. In the corridor he found a telephone and called home, worrying that they would not answer. But Charles did.

'Charles? I'm on top of this building and . . . and a silly thing has happened. Listen – you've got to get me out of here.'

'*You* out! What are you talking about? You've got to get *me* out!' Charles sounded unusually excited.

'What?'

'I'm shut in the pantry. Your dog won't let me out. It's lucky there's a phone in here. You have to come home right away.'

'But I'm in New York! I'm on top of this building and I can't get down!'

'Macon, do you hear that barking? That's Edward. Every time I open the door he attacks me. And now he's attacking the door.'

Macon held the phone tightly. 'Charles, where's Rose?'

'She's out. Julian came to take her to dinner and—'

'Julian my *boss*?'

'Yes, and it's Porter's night for visiting his children. Macon, I can't just sit here waiting for Edward to break through.'

How Macon wished he was safe in the pantry, surrounded by all Rose's groceries lined up in alphabetical order!

'If you don't get me out of this, I'm going to call for the police to come shoot him,' Charles said.

'No! Don't do that! Listen. I'm going to . . . I'll phone Sarah. She'll come over and take charge of Edward. Just wait!'

He hung up and found Sarah's number with trembling hands. But she didn't answer. What now? What on earth now?

He looked through the other numbers in his wallet and saw a name: Muriel Pritchett, animal trainer. She answered at once.

'Muriel?' he said. 'It's Macon Leary.'

'Oh! How're you doing?'

'I'm fine. Or, rather . . .' He tried to explain about Edward and Charles and being on top of a building in New York.

'Let's make sure I've got this right,' Muriel said. 'Edward's in your pantry—'

Macon tried again. 'Edward's *outside* the pantry. My brother's inside, and says he's going to call the police to come shoot Edward so I thought if you could go over and—'

'I'll go right away, and take Edward to the Meow-Bow.'

'Oh, wonderful. And there's something else . . . I'm having this kind of . . . See, I'm on top of this very tall building and I don't know what it is but something has scared the hell out of me.'

'Oh, I think people who go up those buildings are so brave.'

Macon gave a dry laugh, and held the phone more tightly.

'Yes, you ought to be feeling so proud of yourself, just being up there!' she said. 'And Macon, when you get back from your trip, we need to talk about Edward's training. Things just can't go on this way, can they? I mean, this is ridiculous.'

'Yes. Yes, you're absolutely right,' Macon said.

'See you, then. Bye.'

After Macon hung up, he went back into the restaurant and sat down at his table. He felt calm and tired and terribly hungry.

✧   ✧   ✧

'I'll be honest,' Muriel said, 'my baby was not exactly planned for. If you want to know the truth, the baby was the reason I married Norman in the first place. But I didn't push him into it.'

She looked past Macon at Edward, who lay on the hall rug. He'd had to be pushed down, but at least he was staying there.

'Now I'm going to turn my back. You watch how he does.'

She walked into the living room. Macon anxiously watched Edward, and Muriel went on talking. 'My folks didn't want me to get married. Norman and I were just kids, playing at marriage. It was pretend! And then it turned real, and now I've got this great big seven-year-old boy. What's Edward doing now?'

'He's still lying down,' Macon said.

'Maybe tomorrow he'll lie down on his own,' Muriel said. 'You think so?'

'If you practice. If you don't give in. If you don't go all softhearted.' She came close to Macon and touched his arm. 'Never mind,' she told him. 'I think softhearted men are sweet.'

Macon backed away. He just missed stepping on Edward.

✧   ✧   ✧

The lessons continued, as did the history of Muriel's marriage. She talked all the time, and sometimes Macon got the feeling that she used words as a sort of background music. But he couldn't help listening, and was quite shocked when he heard some of the unkind things that Norman's mother had said to Muriel.

'It was the baby that broke our marriage up,' Muriel said. 'Alexander was born early and spent months in the hospital, he was such a sick little baby. Norman wouldn't go near him and he didn't like me spending all my time at the hospital. In the end I took a cleaning job there, to help pay the medical bills, you should have seen them, thousands and thousands of dollars . . .'

She and Macon were walking along the road with Edward, hoping to meet a biker. Edward was getting quite good at lying down and staying, but he still had to learn that he was not allowed to attack bikers.

'If he gives the smallest bark,' Muriel said, 'I'm going to pull his leash so hard he won't know what hit him. It's for his own good, and you've promised not to get upset, remember?'

'Yes, I'll try and remember,' Macon said.

Soon a biker came past, a girl with a tiny, serious face. Edward put his head up and looked, but marched calmly on.

'Oh, Edward, that was wonderful,' Macon told him.

Muriel just clucked, as though she had expected Edward to behave himself.

'So anyhow,' she said. 'They finally let Alexander come home, and a few weeks later Norman just walked out. Packed his clothes and went back to his mother. I knew I couldn't go back to my folks, so I just had to manage. I did all kinds of jobs, sometimes two or three at a time, but it wasn't easy.'

She slowed and then came to a stop. Edward, with a deep sigh, sat down at her left heel. 'Looking back, I almost missed the times in the hospital,' she said. 'The nurses talking and those rows of little babies sleeping. It was winter and sometimes I'd stand at a window, feeling warm and safe, and look down at the emergency room entrance and watch the ambulances coming in. You ever wonder what a Martian would think if he landed near an emergency room? He'd see everybody running out to meet the ambulance, pulling the doors open, hurrying to get the patient inside. "What kind and helpful creatures these are," a Martian would say. Don't you think so?'

She looked up at Macon then. Macon felt something turn over inside him. He felt there was something he needed to do, some connection he wanted to make, and when she raised her face, he bent and kissed her lips, though that wasn't the connection he had intended.

'Well . . .' he said.

She went on looking up at him.

'Sorry,' he said.

Then they turned around and walked Edward home.

✧   ✧   ✧

It was getting close to Thanksgiving and as usual the Learys were discussing Thanksgiving dinner. None of them liked turkey, but in the end they always decided to have it. Porter's three teenage children were coming to stay for Thanksgiving, and Rose thought she might invite Julian Edge too. Poor Julian, she said, was on his own and might enjoy a family dinner.

This alarmed Macon. Julian was often stopping by to take Rose this place or that, and Macon suspected him of amusing himself with another member of the peculiar Leary family. But Julian always behaved very politely with Rose, almost shy, and clumsy about opening doors. Macon hoped that Rose was not having any foolish thoughts about love, but she was so plain and sensible there was surely no need to worry.

On Thanksgiving morning Macon came down to the kitchen where Rose was giving breakfast to Porter's children. He said, 'Rose, I thought I could smell turkey cooking in the night.'

'You could,' Rose said. 'I'm trying this new way of cooking meat. It saves electricity. You set the temperature extremely low and cook the meat all night.'

'But it won't be properly cooked,' Macon said.

'It will murder us,' said Charles.

'You're both wrong,' Rose said. 'It's going to be delicious.'

Maybe it was, but it certainly didn't look it. By dinnertime the middle of the bird had fallen in and the skin was all dry and dull. Rose carried the bird in and put it on the table. 'Ah, look at that!' Julian said enthusiastically. He was the only person at the table who didn't know how the turkey had been cooked.

'Well, there may be a little problem,' Macon said.

Rose looked at him angrily.

'The vegetables are excellent,' he said. 'But the turkey . . .'

'Is just poison,' Danny finished for him. At sixteen, he was the oldest of Porter's children, and already as tall as Porter.

'It's been cooked at too low a temperature,' Macon explained.

'I think it looks delicious,' Julian said.

'Yes,' Porter told him. 'But you don't know about the other times – the chicken salad that was left out all night and . . .'

Rose sat down. Her eyes filled with tears. 'Oh,' she said, 'you're all so mean! You don't fool me for a moment. You're just trying to make me look bad in front of Julian. You know perfectly well there's nothing wrong with that turkey. You just don't want me to stop cooking for you and taking care of this house, you don't want Julian to fall in love with me.'

'Do what?'

But she pushed her chair back and ran from the room. Julian sat there with his mouth open.

'Don't you dare laugh,' Macon told him. 'Don't even think about it.'

Julian swallowed. 'Do you think I should go after her?'

'No. She's fine. Now, who wants a baked potato?'

The three children all asked for baked potatoes with vegetables, and Macon then turned to Julian.

'Julian? Potato?'

'I'll take the turkey,' Julian said firmly.

At that moment Macon almost liked the man.

✧   ✧   ✧

'You want your dog to obey you in every situation,' Muriel said. 'You want to leave him outside shops or any public place and come back and find him waiting. Right, here's a grocery store.'

*'You know perfectly well there's nothing wrong
with that turkey,' Rose said.*

They climbed out of Muriel's old gray car and went over to
the grocery. Macon tapped his foot twice. Edward looked
unhappy, but he lay down. Inside the store Macon and Muriel
walked past the fruit and vegetables. Muriel picked up a banana

and put it down again. 'Too green,' she said. 'What are you doing for dinner tomorrow night? Come and eat at my house.'

'Um . . .'

'Come on. We'll have fun. Just you and me and Alexander. He needs to meet more men, it's good for him.'

'Um, I don't know if I'm free tomorrow . . .'

'Think it over. Six o'clock. Sixteen Singleton Street.'

They went outside. Edward was still there, but standing up and growling at a dog across the street. Muriel sighed.

They tried several more shops, with varying success, then Muriel parked in front of a building in Cold Spring Lane.

'One more test,' she said. 'I've got to pick up Alexander at the doctor's here. It won't take long. You come in with me.'

They left Edward lying down outside and went in.

'How old did you say Alexander was?' Macon asked.

'He's seven,' Muriel said.

Seven. Seven was when Ethan had learned to ride a bicycle.

Alexander was a small, white, sickly boy with short thin hair and light blue eyes behind large watery glasses. Macon shook hands with him. He felt there was nothing on earth he could talk about with this child.

Muriel drove Macon back to his house and as they pulled up outside she said, 'I'll see you tomorrow for dinner then.'

Macon didn't know how to tell her, but he knew he couldn't go to that dinner. He missed his wife. He missed his son. They were the only people who seemed real to him. There was no point looking for anyone to take their places.

6

The invitation

Macon looked up the phone number in the book. It was nine in the evening, a good time to call. Alexander would have gone to bed. He picked up the phone.

But what would he say?

Muriel, last year my son died and I . . . Muriel, this has nothing to do with you personally but . . . Muriel, I can't. I just can't.

He held the phone to his ear but his throat had closed up, his voice had disappeared. He had never actually said out loud that Ethan was dead. He hadn't needed to; it was in the newspapers, and then friends had told other friends.

He hung up.

He found some notepaper, sat down, took out his pen. *Dear Muriel*, he wrote. And stared at the page for a while.

Funny sort of name, Muriel. He examined his pen closely. How well made it was. He examined the notepaper.

Well.

Dear Muriel, I am very sorry, he wrote, *but I won't be able to have dinner with you after all. Something unexpected has happened. Yours, Macon.*

He put the letter in his pocket and drove to the south of the city. He wondered how Muriel could feel safe living here, among these dark streets full of rubbish and young men drinking out of brown paper bags. He turned onto Singleton Street.

He found number 16, got out of the car and climbed the steps.

He opened the screen door and took the letter from his pocket.

'I've got a gun,' Muriel said from inside the house, 'and I'm aiming it exactly where your head is.'

His heart started beating very fast. Her voice sounded level and accurate – like her gun, he imagined. 'It's Macon,' he said.

'Macon?' The inner door opened a little. 'Macon, what are you doing here?'

He gave her the letter.

She took it and opened it, using both hands. (There was no sign of a gun.) She read it and looked up at him.

He saw he had done it all wrong.

'Last year,' he said, 'I lost . . . I experienced a . . . loss, yes.'

She went on looking into his face.

'I lost my son,' Macon said. 'He was . . . at a hamburger bar and then . . . someone came, a gunman, and shot him. I can't go to dinner with people! I can't talk to their little boys! I don't mean to hurt your feelings but I'm just not up to this, do you hear?'

She took one of his wrists very gently and she drew him into the house, still not fully opening the door, so that he had the sense of slipping through something, of narrowly avoiding something. She closed the door behind him. She put her arms around him and hugged him.

'Every day I tell myself it's time to be getting over this,' he said into the space above her head. 'I know that people expect it of me. They used to offer their sympathy but now they don't; they don't even mention his name. They think it's time my life moved on. The first year was like a bad dream – I was at his bedroom door in the morning before I remembered he wasn't there to be woken. But this second year is worse, it's real. I've stopped going to his door. I've sometimes let a whole day pass without thinking about him. And you'd suppose Sarah and I could comfort each other but no, we only do each other harm. I think this has only brought out the truth about us – how far apart we are. And now I'm far from everyone; I don't have any friends anymore and everyone looks silly and foolish and not related to me.'

She drew him through a living room, up a stairway and across a hall and into a bedroom.

'No,' he said, 'wait. This is not what I want.'

'Just sleep,' she told him. 'Lie down and sleep.'

That seemed reasonable.

She removed his coat and hung it in a closet. She knelt and untied his shoes. He stepped out of them obediently. She hung his trousers and shirt over a chair back. He dropped onto the bed in his underwear, and she drew the cover over him.

Next he heard her moving through the rest of the house, turning off lights, running water, saying something in another room. She returned to the bedroom. Her robe was old, made of silk, the color of red wine. Then she got into bed and lay close to him. 'I just want to sleep,' he told her. But there was this silk material next to him. He felt how cool and soft the silk was, cool silk over warm body.

✧　　✧　　✧

In the night he heard a child cough, and he swam up through a sea of dreams to answer. But he was in a room with one tall blue window, and the child was not Ethan. He turned over and found Muriel. She sighed in her sleep, a soft sound full of remembered pain, which seemed to say to Macon, *About your son . . . I am wounded too. We're all wounded. You are not the only one.*

7

Life on Singleton Street

'I don't understand you,' Rose told Macon. 'First you say you'll be here, and then you say you won't. How can I plan meals when you are so disorganized?'

'Sorry, Rose,' Macon said.

'Last night you weren't here to eat your supper. Three separate mornings these past two weeks I go to call you for breakfast and I find you haven't slept in your bed. Don't you think I worry?'

'Well, sometimes I don't realize how late it's getting and . . .'

'I'm not asking about your private life,' Rose said.

'I thought in a way you were.'

'I just need to know how many breakfasts to fix.'

'You think I don't notice what's going on? Whenever she's here giving Edward his lesson, everyone starts coming out of the woodwork. Porter, edging through the living room – "Just looking for a hammer! Don't mind me!" You, coming out to sweep the porch the minute we go outside . . .'

'Could I help it if the porch was dirty?'

'Well, I'll be here tomorrow night for supper. That's certain.'

Although even as he spoke, he heard how false and shallow he sounded, and he saw how Rose lowered her eyes.

✧　　✧　　✧

He bought a huge pizza and drove downtown with it. The smell made him so hungry that he kept eating bits off the top. Whistling softly, he drove through the back streets and turned onto Singleton.

46

The next-door neighbor's twin daughters, Debbie and Dorrie Butler, were sitting by their front door – sixteen-year-olds in jeans as tight as a second skin. 'Hey there, Macon,' they called out.

'How are you, girls?'

Macon gave them a big smile. They sometimes sat with Alexander when Muriel was out; he had to be nice to them. Half the neighborhood sat with Alexander, it seemed. He still felt confused by Muriel's arrangements.

It was Alexander who opened the door. 'Mama's on the phone,' he said flatly, and went back to watching TV.

'It's pizza night,' Macon told him.

'I'm allergic to pizza.'

'You can't be allergic to all of it.'

'Well, I am.'

Muriel had told him that Alexander was allergic to milk, fruit, eggs, and most vegetables; also to dust and paint, and possibly to air. He had breathing problems, and suffered from skin complaints and nosebleeds. He was always having to have injections for one thing or another.

Macon went on into the kitchen. Muriel stood with her back to him, talking on the phone with her mother. He could tell it was her mother because of Muriel's high, sad, complaining voice. 'Aren't you going to ask how Alexander is? I ask after *your* health, Ma, why don't you ask about ours?'

He presented himself in front of her, holding out the pizza. She looked up at him, and gave that quick, bright smile of hers – a cheerful V in her pointed little face.

'Ma,' she said. 'I'm going now! Macon's here!'

It had been a long, long time since anyone had made such an event of his arrival.

❖   ❖   ❖

He went to Julian's office on a Monday afternoon and handed over the work he'd done on the U.S. guidebook. 'That's the Northeast done,' he said. 'I guess next I'll start on the South.'

'Good,' Julian said. He was looking through a drawer in his desk. 'Excellent. Like to show you something, Macon.' He gave Macon a tiny blue box. 'Your sister's Christmas present,' he said.

Macon raised the lid. Inside, on a bed of white silk, was a diamond ring. He looked at Julian.

'What is it?' he asked.

'What *is* it? It's an engagement ring, Macon.'

'Engagement?'

'I want to marry her.'

'You want to marry Rose?'

'What's so odd about that?'

'Well, I—' Macon said.

'I'll ask her at Christmas, when I give her the ring. I want to do this properly. Do you think she'll have me?'

'Well, I really couldn't say.' Unfortunately, Macon was sure she would, but he didn't see why he should tell Julian that.

'She's got to,' Julian said. 'I'm thirty-six years old, Macon, but I tell you, I feel like a schoolboy about that woman. She's everything that most modern girls are not. She's so . . . true. I want to do everything right. What do you think of the ring?'

'It's okay.' Macon looked down at it. Then he said, 'It's very nice, Julian,' and he closed the box gently and handed it back.

✧　　✧　　✧

Above all else Macon was an orderly man. He was happiest with routine, and regular arrangements repeated over and over. Buying groceries on the same day each week, paying bills on another. There was no room in his life for someone as changeable as Muriel. Or as extreme. Or as . . . well, unlikable, sometimes.

She was so much younger than he was. She made him anxious about his age, his stiffness after sitting a long time, and the way he was always expecting his bad back to give him trouble again. And she talked so much – about the appearance of things, her hair, her skin, the color of clothes.

Yet he knew that what mattered was the pattern of her life; that although he did not love her he loved the surprise of her, and also the surprise of himself when he was with her. In the foreign country that was Singleton Street he was a completely different person. This person had never been suspected of narrowness, never been accused of being cold and without feeling; in fact, was laughed at for his soft heart. And was anything but orderly.

He spent more and more time in Singleton Street. One day Muriel asked him, 'Why don't you come to my folks' house for Christmas dinner? I want you to meet them.'

They were in the kitchen, and Macon was trying to teach Alexander how to fix a faucet.

'Oh, well, I don't know,' he said.

'Please say yes, Macon! Ma thinks I've invented you. You know how she is.'

Yes, Macon did know, at least from listening to Muriel's telephone conversations with her mother. The fact was, he just didn't want to get involved. So instead of answering, he concentrated on Alexander.

'Why did I turn off the water under the sink, Alexander?'

Alexander said, 'Why.'

'You tell me.'

'You tell *me*.'

'No, you,' Macon said firmly.

There was a bad moment or two when it seemed that Alexander might go on staring glassily forever. Finally he said,

'So the water from the faucet won't whoosh all over.'

'Right. Now the leak is here, in the handle, so you want to take the handle apart and replace the packing. First you unscrew the top screw. Let's see you do it.'

'Me?' Alexander shook his head. 'I don't want to.'

'Let him just watch,' Muriel suggested.

'If he just watches, he won't learn how to do it.'

Slowly, Alexander took the screwdriver that Macon was holding out to him, climbed onto a chair, and breathing heavily, began to undo the screw with the screwdriver. It took him forever. With each turn, the screwdriver slipped out and had to be repositioned. At last, however, the screw was out.

'Wonderful,' Macon said. 'I believe you may have a natural ability for this.'

Muriel, watching silently for once, became less anxious. 'What do you like for your Christmas dinner, Macon? A turkey? Or something else? You can tell me! My folks won't mind!'

Alexander was getting on well. He put in the new packing for the handle and slowly put the faucet back together.

'Now what,' he ordered.

'Now we turn the water back on and see if the leak has gone,' Macon said. He showed Alexander where to turn the water on under the sink, and then he turned on the faucet. No leak.

'Look at that!' he told Alexander. 'You've solved the problem. Now when you're grown, you can fix the faucets for your wife.'

Alexander found this idea amusing, and made his funny little laughing noise. 'Tssh!' he said. 'Tssh!'

'Macon? Are you coming to my folks', or not?' Muriel asked.

It seemed unreasonable to say he wasn't. Somehow or other, he had got himself involved already.

✧   ✧   ✧

Muriel's parents lived in Timonium, right out on the edge of town. When they arrived at the house, a well-built, pretty teenager in blue jeans ran out to meet them.

'Claire!' Alexander shouted, waving at her from the car.

'That's my sister,' Muriel told Macon.

Macon gathered up all the presents for Muriel's family, and Alexander took his toolbox from the backseat. This was Macon's Christmas present to him – a box full of tools, small enough for a child, but real, with solid wooden handles.

They followed Claire into the house. Mrs Dugan, Muriel's mother, was a small, thin, gray woman. She greeted her daughter and grandson without much enthusiasm, and studied Macon carefully. 'Pleased to meet you,' she said finally.

Mr Dugan came in, shook Macon's hand, and went out again. 'He's worried about the pipes in the basement freezing up in this cold weather,' Mrs Dugan explained.

'Oh, could I help?' Macon asked, interested.

'Now, you just sit right where you are, Mr Leary.'

'Macon,' he said.

'Macon. Well, Macon, Muriel tells me you're separated.'

'Um, yes, I am.'

'What about the future, then?'

'Pardon?'

'I mean, you're not just taking Muriel for a ride, are you?'

'Ma, stop that,' Muriel said.

'Well, I wouldn't have to ask, Muriel, if you had ever had any common sense yourself. This girl was only thirteen years old,' Mrs Dugan told Macon, 'when she was running around with all kinds of wild boys. I haven't had a good night's sleep since.'

'Well, I don't know why not,' Muriel said. 'That was years and years ago. Ma, why don't you open your present?'

'But you never did get it right, did you? There was that Dr Kane from the Meow-Bow. He was single, and a professional man. I had high hopes for him,' Mrs Dugan said sadly.

'Ma, will you please just open your Christmas present?'

'Oh, did you bring me a present?'

Muriel fetched her gift from under the Christmas tree and handed it to her mother. Mrs Dugan unwrapped it. It was a photograph in a gold-painted frame. She stared at it.

'Well, isn't that nice,' Mrs Dugan said.

'Well, isn't that nice,' she said finally. She turned it toward Macon. The photo was in soft dreamy colors and gentle lighting, and showed Muriel seated, with Alexander standing in front of her. Neither of them smiled. They looked watchful and uncertain, and very much alone.

Macon said, 'It's beautiful.'

'Hmm,' Mrs Dugan said, and laid the photo on the table.

Mr Dugan reappeared for dinner and became quite talkative. He was a car salesman and had firm opinions on what car Macon should be driving. Listening to him, and to Muriel and her mother arguing about Alexander's health problems, Macon wondered what Sarah would say if she could see him here. Or Rose and his brothers. He knew what Julian would say. 'Ha! *Accidental Tourist in Timonium*.'

Back home that evening, they sat in the living room.

'I know what you must be thinking,' Muriel said. 'You're thinking this Muriel is just on the lookout for anybody in trousers. I expect you want to stop seeing me.'

'Why would I want to stop seeing you?'

'After how bad Ma made me look.'

'You didn't look bad.'

'Oh, no?'

'Last Christmas,' Macon said, 'was very hard to get through. It was the first one without Ethan. We didn't know what to do, and we got it all wrong. It was a terrible Christmas.'

He smoothed Muriel's hair off her forehead. 'This one was better,' he said.

8

The wrong type of woman

Macon began to spend all his time at Muriel's house, to pay his share toward her rent and her groceries. He kept his shaving things in her bathroom and hung his clothes in her closet. He fetched his typewriter and worked at the kitchen table so that he could be around when Alexander was home alone.

The final thing was Edward. Macon returned from a business trip, and Rose told him, 'Edward spends all his time in the hall, staring at the door, waiting for you to come back.'

That did it. He brought Edward back with him when he returned to Singleton Street. There were worries that the dog hair would be bad for Alexander's allergies, but in the end it didn't seem to make any difference.

Edward was wildly happy. He rushed madly all over the house, enthusiastically licked Muriel's hands, and developed an immediate interest in Alexander, inviting him to throw balls and lying next to him on the couch when Alexander watched TV.

In the mornings Macon started fixing breakfast for Alexander, eggs and hot milk. Alexander then walked to school with Buddy and Sissy Ebbetts, two tough-looking older children from across the street. Muriel left for one or other of her jobs, depending on what day it was.

The days took on a regular pattern. Macon worked at his latest guidebook in the morning, writing and arranging future trips. Sometimes he did a few repairs around the house – there was so much that needed fixing! As he worked, he often

54

wondered about Muriel, feeling a strong curiosity about her inner thoughts. She never attempted to hide her true nature from him, which was certainly far from perfect. She had a nasty temper, a sharp tongue, and could fall into deep depressions for hours. She was obviously intelligent, but at the same time she firmly believed that you could tell the future from dreams. She also believed in fortune-telling, knew that her magic number was seventeen, and in a previous life had been a fashion designer.

At three o'clock Alexander got home from school, letting himself in with a key tied on a string around his neck.

'How was your day?' Macon always asked.

'Oh, okay.'

But Macon had the feeling that school never went very well for Alexander. His glasses were always covered in fingerprints, and his face seemed paler than ever. Sometimes Macon helped him with his schoolwork, simple questions about his reading. 'Why did Joe need five dollars? Where was Joe's daddy?'

'Umm . . .' Alexander said, staring anxiously at the page.

'Take your time,' Macon told him. 'There's no hurry.'

'But I can't! I don't know! I don't know!'

Macon felt tied to Alexander in all sorts of complicated ways, but he could still draw back from him, he was not responsible for him. It was a comfort to know that.

When Muriel came home, she brought fresh air and action and excitement. 'Is it ever cold! Is it ever windy! Radio says three below zero tonight. Edward, down, this minute. Who wants lemon cake tonight? Here's what happened in my day . . .'

As she talked, she moved around the kitchen getting supper. Later, she talked to her mother on the phone or, more usually, to her sister Claire, who was apparently having troubles at home.

'Tell them!' Muriel advised her. 'Tell them you're not a kid any more. You're seventeen years old and you can do what you like.'

Her girlfriend might drop by after supper – a fat young woman named Bernice who worked for the Gas Company. Or neighbors might knock on the kitchen door. 'Muriel, Saturday I got to go to the hospital, any chance of you giving me a lift?'

Muriel was unusual on this street in having a car, which was only possible through a complicated arrangement with a boy down the street, who was a good mechanic. The agreement was that Dominick did all the repairs on the car, and Muriel let him have the use of it three nights a week and all day Sunday.

Macon felt at peace on Singleton Street. He liked everything exactly the way it was, and wanted nothing to change.

✧　　✧　　✧

On Wednesday there was a heavy snowstorm, and the next day Macon woke late, to a white, silent world. The snow was four feet deep, and the radio news said that schools were closed, factories were closed, nobody was going anywhere.

Downstairs the kitchen was full of people. Claire was cooking pancakes, Alexander was eating them, Muriel was sitting with her cup of coffee, and Bernice was standing inside the back door, dripping snow. Claire had been sleeping on the couch for the last few nights, having walked out after an argument with her mother. 'I told Ma,' she was telling Bernice, 'I'd had enough of all her moaning – where had I been, who was I with, on and on and on!'

Then she saw Macon. 'Hey there, Macon. Want a pancake?'

'Just a glass of milk, thanks.'

'No newspaper this morning,' Alexander told Macon. 'Edward's going crazy, waiting for it to come.'

A figure appeared at the back door, and Edward started barking. Macon opened the door and found his brother Charles.

'Charles?' he said. 'What are you doing here?'

Charles stepped in, bringing the smell of new snow. 'Your neighbor Garner Bolt called and said pipes have burst in your house, water all over everything. I've been trying to phone you but it's always busy.'

'That was me,' Claire said. 'Wanted to stop my folks calling.'

'This is Muriel's sister, Claire,' Macon said, 'and that's Alexander and that's Bernice. My brother Charles.'

Charles looked confused. He refused one of Claire's pancakes but accepted a glass of milk from Muriel, and when Macon had fetched his coat, seemed glad to make his escape.

They drove carefully through the snowy streets to Macon's house. The living room was a disaster area – bits of ceiling had fallen down, and all over the room it was raining, water running down the walls, through the curtains, pools lying on the floor.

Charles was shocked. 'What are you going to *do*?' he said.

'Turn off the water in the basement,' Macon said. 'Find my boots, and go.' The ruin of his living room did not upset him. It belonged to another life, a different person. It was the past.

When they were back in the car, Charles turned to Macon with a serious expression. 'I think it's time we had a talk,' he said.

'What about?'

'This Muriel person. Everybody says that—'

'Is that what you call her – "this Muriel person"?'

'No one else will tell you. They say it's none of their business,' Charles said. 'But I can't just stand by and watch. Macon, she's, well . . . she's not your type of woman.'

'You don't even know her!'

'I know her type. You're not yourself these days – we can all see it, Porter, Rose, me . . .'

'You're all so good at running your own lives, of course.'

'We're just worried for you, Macon. This Muriel person is just

57

not worth ruining your life for. Can you tell me one really special thing about her? Not something silly like "She listens to me."'

She looks out of hospital windows and imagines how the Martians would see us, Macon wanted to say. But Charles wouldn't understand that, so he said, 'I'm not so special myself, in case you haven't noticed. Damaged is the word, probably.'

'That's not true. She's lucky to have caught you. She'd be lucky to find anyone, in fact. She doesn't speak proper English, she lives in that awful house, she wears cheap, nasty clothes, she has that sickly little boy who looks like—'

'Charles, just shut the hell up,' Macon said.

When they got close to Singleton Street, Macon said goodbye to Charles, left the car and walked home.

Freedom! Sunlight shining on white snow, children throwing snowballs, boys clearing steps and paths. And then Muriel's house, with its small rooms smelling of pancakes, its crowd of women in the kitchen. They were drinking hot chocolate now. Bernice was combing out Claire's hair. Alexander was painting a picture. Muriel kissed Macon hello. 'Ooh! Your face is so cold. Come in and get warm. Have some hot chocolate.'

✧   ✧   ✧

'I'm sorry I'm so fat,' the man said. He was sitting next to Macon in the airplane. 'Really I ought to buy tickets for two seats and not spread all over other passengers, but I'm not a wealthy man.'

'It's okay,' Macon said. 'It's not a problem.'

'And I travel for a living, too,' the man said. 'Computers. I'm in an airplane seat six days out of seven sometimes.' He held out his hand to Macon. 'Name's Lucas Loomis.'

'Macon Leary,' Macon said.

'What do you do, Mr Leary?'

'I write guidebooks for businessmen. People like you, I guess.'

'*Accidental Tourist*,' Mr Loomis said immediately.

'Why, yes.'

'Really? Am I right? Well, what do you know,' Mr Loomis said. 'Look at this.' He pointed to his suit. 'Gray suit, suitable for all occasions. I take your books on all my trips. The advice is always great. Sometimes I feel I haven't even left home!'

'Well, good,' Macon said. He was on a flight back to Baltimore from San Francisco, a city new to him, which he had found rather beautiful. He mentioned this to Mr Loomis.

'I was born and raised in Baltimore, myself,' Mr Loomis said. 'Wouldn't live anywhere else for the world.'

'No, of course not,' Macon said. 'I just meant—'

'Couldn't pay me to leave it.'

'No, me either.'

'You a Baltimore man?'

'Yes, certainly.'

'No place like it.'

'Certainly isn't,' Macon said.

But a picture came into his mind of San Francisco floating on mist, viewed from a street so high and steep that you could hang your head over and hear the wind blow.

When he got back to Baltimore, spring was in the air and the trees were touched with green. Outside the house Dominick was working on Muriel's car, watched by the Butler twins. Macon stopped to talk to them, then went into the house. He walked through the untidy rooms and thought (not for the first time) that the world was sharply divided down the middle. Some lived careful lives and some lived careless lives, and everything that happened could be explained by the difference between them.

He decided to take Edward out for a walk, and as he was

returning, he saw Alexander ahead of him, on his way home from school. 'Wait!' he was crying out. 'Wait for me!' The Ebbetts children, some distance away, turned and called something back. Macon couldn't hear the words, but the voices were high and cruel. Alexander started running, clumsy in his heavy shoes. Behind him a group of older children also started calling out and laughing. Alexander turned and looked at them. His face was somehow smaller than usual.

'Go,' Macon told Edward, and he dropped the leash.

Edward flew down the street. The older children ran away as he rushed at them, barking. He stopped suddenly in front of Alexander, and Alexander knelt down to hug his neck.

When Macon arrived, he said, 'Are you all right?'

Alexander nodded and got to his feet.

'What was all that about?' Macon asked him.

Alexander said, 'Nothing.' But when they started walking again, he slipped his hand into Macon's.

Macon held those cool little fingers in his, and felt a pleasant kind of sadness running through him. Oh, danger had returned to his life. He was forced to worry once again about wars and disasters and the future of the world.

✧   ✧   ✧

Julian stopped by to discuss the U.S. guides for the West Coast. It seemed an unnecessary visit to Macon – no doubt the real purpose was to spy – and he kept Julian in the living room. The others were all in the kitchen, and Macon had no intention of letting Julian meet them.

But Julian said, 'Aren't you going to introduce me to Muriel?'

'She's busy.'

'I'd really like to meet her.'

'Why? Hasn't Rose given you a full report?'

'Are you all right?' Macon said.

'Macon,' Julian said, 'when I marry Rose, I'll be your brother-in-law. It's only natural that I want to know Muriel. Anyway, I want to invite her to the wedding. So can I talk to her?'

'Oh. Well. I guess so.'

In the kitchen Muriel, Claire, and Bernice were seated round the table, looking at a notebook. Macon introduced everybody.

'Hello, ladies,' Julian said cheerfully. 'I've come to invite you to my wedding, Muriel. And your little boy.'

'Oh, well . . . er, thank you.' Muriel waved the ballpoint pen she was holding. 'We're working on this song for a country-music competition,' she told Julian. 'We could win a trip for two to Nashville. Listen.' She began to sing in a high, scratchy voice.

When we kissed in the rain, when we shared every pain,
When we both enjoyed happier days.

'Very good,' Julian said. 'But I don't know about 'shared every pain'. I mean, in happier days they had pain?'

'He's right,' Bernice told Muriel.

'Rain, plane, main, contain,' Julian said. 'How about, *When we traveled by train, when all of life was a game . . .*'

'I'm sure you've got other things to do, Julian,' Macon said.

'*When I hadn't met Jane, when she didn't know Wayne . . .*'

'Wait!' Bernice said, writing it down as fast as she could.

'I'll see you to the door,' Macon said to Julian.

'*When her face was so plain, when our love had no stain . . .*' Julian said, following Macon out to the hall. 'Don't forget the wedding!' he called back to Muriel. To Macon he said, 'I'm taking Rose to Hawaii. Do you think she'll like it?'

'I know nothing at all about Hawaii,' Macon said.

At the front door Julian stopped. 'She may be exactly what you need, this Muriel person,' he said. 'She's not so bad! I don't think your family understands how you're feeling.'

'No, they don't. They really don't,' Macon said. He was surprised it was Julian, of all people, who saw that.

Julian's final words were, '*When we drank wine from Spain . . .*', and Macon shut the door firmly behind him.

9

The wedding

On the day of the wedding Macon woke to the sound of rain falling on the roof. The ceremony was going to take place in the Learys' garden and Macon's first thought was 'Poor Rose!' He went downstairs and phoned her.

'Are you moving the wedding indoors?' he asked her.

'No, we've got too many guests. Never mind, it will clear.'

'But the grass is all wet!'

'Wear boots,' she told him, and hung up.

Since she'd met Julian she'd grown so light-hearted, Macon thought. So carefree. Not a serious person anymore.

She was right about the weather, though. By afternoon there was sunshine. Muriel wore a pretty, summery dress. She wanted Alexander to put on a suit, but both he and Macon protested.

'Jeans and a good white shirt will be fine,' Macon told her.

'Well, if you're sure.'

Lately, she had been following his advice about Alexander. He was now allowed to wear blue jeans and T-shirts like other boys. He ate all kinds of food and rarely seemed to suffer from any of his former allergies. His face was not so thin and pale, and his hair, which Macon cut for him, was growing thicker.

The first person they saw when they arrived was Macon's mother, come to see her daughter married. For some reason this took Macon by surprise, and for a moment he wondered who Alicia was. 'Macon, dear!' she said. She had not changed much, Macon thought, except her hair was now a deeper, richer red.

They went through to the backyard, where there were spring flowers set everywhere in buckets, and a huge crowd of people. It seemed that everybody Macon had ever known was there.

'If you have back pain,' Charles was telling the family doctor, 'I'm told it's best to sleep on the floor . . .'

Porter's ex-wife June was talking to Muriel about having babies. Julian was asking Alicia about her travels in South America. A neighbor was telling the mailman that Leary Metals was the oldest family business in Baltimore.

And Sarah was talking to Macon about the weather.

He said something about the rain, something or other, while he watched her shiny curls and her round, sweet face.

'How have you been, Macon?' she asked him.

'I've been all right.'

'Are you pleased about the wedding?'

'Well,' he said, 'I am if Rose is, I guess.' In the sunlight her eyes were so clear it seemed you could see to the backs of them.

'How have *you* been?' he said.

'I've been fine.'

'Well. Good.'

'I know that you're living with someone,' she said quietly. She looked past him at Muriel and Alexander. 'Rose told me.'

He said, 'How about you?'

'Me?'

'Are you living with anyone?'

'Not really.'

Then they were called for the ceremony and Macon went to his position. Sarah stood opposite him, looking into his face.

It all felt so natural.

10

The phone call

Muriel said, 'I never told you this, but a while before I met you, I nearly married somebody else. He was divorced and really miserable, but over the months I helped him get through it. We started talking about getting married. Then he met this girl and went off and married her within a week.'

'I see,' Macon said.

'You wouldn't do anything like that, would you, Macon?'

'Oh, Muriel, of course not,' he told her.

'Would you leave me and go home to your wife?'

'What are you talking about?'

'Would you?'

'Don't be silly.'

She put her head on one side and looked at him, with her bright, knowing eyes.

A few days later they were out shopping, in one of Muriel's favorite thrift shops. She bought all kinds of things from thrift shops and most of her clothes and shoes. Macon had even begun to like thrift shops himself, as among all the plastic rubbish he sometimes found interesting old tools.

'Look,' Muriel said. She was holding an old brown suitcase. 'Should I get this?'

'What for? You don't need it.'

'I know where you're going next,' she said. 'After Canada, I mean. Julian said it was time for you to go to France again. I wanted to ask if I could come with you.'

'You know I can't afford to take you.'

'But just this once. It wouldn't cost much! I've always wanted to go to France.'

Macon looked through the window at Edward outside the shop. 'Muriel, I think Edward's getting restless now,' he said.

Muriel replaced the suitcase and they left the shop. But France did not go away. Over the next few days Muriel sent him a letter put together from magazine print: **Don't FoRget tO BUY pLANe TickET for MuRieL**. She left two passport photos of herself lying on the kitchen table for a week.

Macon liked her determination. Had he ever known such a fighter? Life had not been kind to her, but she never gave in. She just lifted her pointed little chin, and went on fighting.

One evening before supper he said to her, 'I don't think Alexander is getting a proper education. He can't do even simple adding up. I think he ought to go to a private school.'

'Private schools cost money,' Muriel said.

'So? I'll pay.'

Muriel stopped cutting up tomatoes and looked at him. 'What are you saying?' she asked.

'Pardon?'

'What are you saying, Macon? Alexander's got ten more years of school ahead of him. Are you saying that you're going to be around for all ten years?'

'Um . . .'

'I can't put him in a school and take him out again if you go.' He was silent.

'Tell me,' she said. 'Do you see us getting married sometime?' He said, 'Oh, well, marriage, Muriel . . .'

'You don't, do you? You don't know *what* you want. One minute you like me and the next you don't. One minute you're ashamed to be seen with me and the next you think I'm the best thing that ever happened to you.'

He stared at her. He had never guessed that she read him so clearly.

'Maybe tomorrow you'll be here, maybe you won't. Maybe you'll just go on back to Sarah. Oh yes! Don't think I didn't see how you and Sarah looked at each other at Rose's wedding.'

'All I'm saying is I want Alexander to learn to add up!'

'All *I'm* saying,' Muriel said, 'is take care what you promise my son. Don't go making him promises you don't intend to keep.'

At supper she was too quiet. Alexander was also quiet, and quickly disappeared when the meal was over. Muriel began to wash the dishes at the sink. Macon said, 'Shall I dry?' Without any warning, Muriel turned and threw a wet cloth in his face.

'Just get out!' she shouted, tears shining in her eyes.

Macon went away and watched TV with Alexander. Later, he cautiously returned to the kitchen, where Muriel was talking to her mother on the phone. He came up behind her and put his arms around her, and she leaned back against him.

✧   ✧   ✧

The mailman rang the doorbell and gave Macon a large stiff, brown envelope addressed to him. He took it into the living room where Muriel was sitting, reading.

'This looks like your handwriting on the envelope,' he said.

Muriel turned a page of her book.

He opened the envelope and found a calendar. Puzzled, he looked through the months – January, February, March, April, May. Then June. A word in red ink written across a Saturday. 'Wedding,' he read out. 'Wedding? Whose wedding?'

'Ours?' she asked him.

'Oh, Muriel . . .'

'Just get out!' Muriel shouted.

'You'll be separated a year then, Macon. You can get your divorce. I always did want to have a June wedding.'

'Muriel, please, I'm not ready for this! I don't think I ever will be. I mean, I don't think people should get married. Well, perfect couples could marry, maybe, but who's a perfect couple?'

'You and Sarah, I suppose,' Muriel said.

'No, no . . .' he said weakly.

'You're so selfish!' Muriel shouted. 'So self-centered! You've got all these clever reasons for never doing a single thing I want!'

Then she threw down her book and ran upstairs.

Macon heard the cautious sounds of Alexander as he very quietly got himself a drink from the kitchen.

✧   ✧   ✧

Muriel's sister Claire arrived on the doorstep with a suitcase full of clothes and her eyes pink with tears. 'I'm never speaking to Ma again,' she told them. She pushed past them into the house. 'You want to know what happened?'

There followed a long complicated story about Claire's latest boyfriend and the arguments Claire was having with her mother, who had got completely the wrong idea about the boyfriend and believed, for no clear reason, that he was a General in the army. 'And then she says,' Claire went on, 'that I can't ever see the General again or she'll have him drummed out of the army, so I rush upstairs and pack up all my clothes . . .'

Macon, listening to this story while Edward sighed at his feet, suddenly saw how rich and full and interesting his life was. He would have liked to tell someone about it.

But the person he would have liked to tell was Sarah.

✧   ✧   ✧

A few days before Macon's trip to Canada, Rose and Julian, now back from Hawaii, gave a family supper in their new apartment. Macon and Muriel were invited, and arrived at exactly the same time as Charles and Porter. Muriel wore a quiet gray dress, and her hair was tied back in a neat, tidy way. It was completely unlike her; only her high-heeled, pointy shoes seemed her own.

Everyone told Muriel it was nice to see her, and when at some point in the evening she used an incorrect word, Macon swallowed and stared at the carpet. He waited for someone to correct her, as was the usual Leary habit. But nobody did.

In bed that night Muriel said, 'You wouldn't ever leave me, would you? Would you ever think of leaving me? You won't be like the others, will you? Will you promise not to leave me?'

'Yes, yes,' he said, floating in and out of dreams.

'You do take me seriously, don't you? Don't you?'

'Oh, Muriel . . .'

✧   ✧   ✧

Macon was sitting in a hotel room in Winnipeg, Canada, when the phone rang. It confused him. No one had his number, so far as he knew. He picked up the receiver and said, 'Yes?'

'Macon.'

His heart gave a sudden jump. 'Sarah?'

'Julian thought you'd be staying in this hotel, and I just wanted to ask you . . . Would it be all right with you if I moved back into our house?'

'Um . . .'

'Just for a little while,' she said quickly. 'I have to leave my apartment and I can't find a new one.'

'But the house got flooded, and the ceiling came down—'

'Yes, I know. Your brothers told me.'

'My brothers?'

'They wouldn't answer their phone so I went to ask them where you were, and Rose said the house was—'

'You went to Rose's place, too?'

'No, Rose was at your brothers' house. She's living there for a while.'

'I see,' he said. Then he said, 'She's what?'

'Well, Porter's children are staying there because of some

problem with Porter's ex-wife June. And when Rose heard that, she told Porter she was coming home.'

Sarah had begun to sound like her old self, Macon thought. There was a friendly, smiley sound to her voice. He leaned back against the pillows on his bed.

'But does Rose think Porter can't open a tin of soup for his children?' he said.

'She says Porter and Charles aren't eating right themselves. And there's a crack in the house wall she wants to get fixed.'

'What kind of crack?' Macon asked.

'Some little crack in the stone; I don't know. Water gets in, apparently. And Rose says Porter and Charles were planning to fix it, but they couldn't agree on the best way to do it.'

Macon kicked his shoes off and put his feet up on the bed.

'So is Julian living alone now, or what?'

'Yes, but Rose brings him hot dinners,' Sarah said. Then she said, 'So, is it all right about my using the house, Macon?'

'Oh. It's fine by me, but there's an awful lot of damage—'

'I can get all that done, it's not a problem.' There was a pause. 'Actually, the papers came through from the lawyer,' she said.

'Ah.'

'The final arrangements. You know. Things I have to sign.'

'Yes.'

'It was kind of a shock. I mean of course I knew they were coming; it's been nearly a year. But when I saw them, they seemed so . . . cold, unfeeling. I wasn't expecting that.'

Macon had a sense of some danger rushing toward him, something he could not manage. He said, 'Ah! Yes! Certainly! Very natural. So anyway, good luck with the house, Sarah.'

He hung up quickly.

✧   ✧   ✧

On the flight to Edmonton he sat next to an old woman who was scared of flying. She was so desperate with fear that Macon had to laugh and joke with her, and make encouraging remarks all the time. He could not remember ever having been so bright and cheerful on a flight.

In Edmonton Sarah phoned him to tell him that there was only one burst pipe and it was going to be quite easy to fix. She had begun the cleaning up, she said, but was curious to know why some of the sheets were sewn in half.

In Vancouver she phoned again. 'Well, I've moved back into the house,' she said. 'Mostly I just stay upstairs. The cat and I. I went and picked the cat up at Rose's. I needed company. You wouldn't believe how lonely it is.'

Yes, he would believe it, he could have said. But didn't.

So here they were in their same old positions. He wasn't surprised when she said, 'Macon? Do you . . . What's her name? – Muriel . . . Do you plan on staying with Muriel forever?'

'I really couldn't say,' he said.

How strange the name Muriel sounded, suddenly.

After he landed in Baltimore, he went to his car and drove to the city. It was late evening, with a clear, pale sky. He came to Singleton Street and put his signal on but didn't turn. After a while the signal turned itself off on its own. He rode on through the city, into his old neighborhood. He parked and sat looking at the house. There was a soft light in the upstairs windows. It seemed he had come home.

11

Back home

Macon and Sarah needed to buy a new couch. They decided to go and look for it on Saturday morning, because Sarah had an art class in the afternoon. Before they left Macon took the dog out for a quick walk.

Neighbors were out cutting their grass and tidying their flower beds. He wondered how many of those neat gardens were hiding lives as confused and untidy as his own. Going down to Muriel's, for example, once he'd decided to move back home. He'd had to get his dog, collect his clothes, pack up his typewriter, while Muriel had watched him with sad, accusing eyes.

'Macon? Are you really doing this?' she had said. 'Do you mean to tell me you can just use a person up and then move on? You think I'm some kind of . . . bottle of something you don't have any further need for? Is that how you see me?'

There were things that he'd forgotten – clothes that had been in the wash, his favorite dictionary. More untidiness. But of course he couldn't go back for them.

By the time he and Edward returned, Sarah was waiting in the front yard. She looked very pretty in her yellow summer dress.

'After the furniture store,' she said, 'we must pick up those plants for the garden that Rose promised us.'

It did not take long to buy the couch. 'Should we have a high one? A low one?' Sarah said. 'One that opens into a bed?'

'It's all the same to me,' Macon said. He sat down heavily on something covered in leather.

Sarah chose a long, low, pale green couch. 'What do you think, Macon?' she asked. 'Or do you prefer the one you're sitting on?'

'No, no. The green one is fine.'

'Don't you have any opinion?'

'I just gave you my opinion, Sarah.'

Sarah sighed, and asked the salesman about delivery. When the business was completed, Macon drove on to his grandfather's house, where they found Rose doing some gardening.

Sarah said, 'Where are Porter's children today?'

'Oh, they went home to their mother.'

Sarah said, 'But you haven't moved back with Julian yet?'

'Well, not yet,' Rose said.

'Why? What's keeping you?' Sarah said.

'Oh, Sarah, you wouldn't believe what the boys were like when I came back,' Rose said. 'They were living in their nightclothes so as not to have too much laundry. They were having tinned soup every night for their supper.'

'But what about your apartment, Rose? What about Julian?'

'Oh, you know, I kept losing that apartment somehow,' Rose said absently. 'Every time I went out for groceries, I couldn't seem to find my way back.'

There was a silence. Finally Macon said, 'Well, if you could get us those plants, Rose . . .'

❖ ❖ ❖

They had lunch at the Old Bay Restaurant – Sarah's choice.

'But you always tell me it's boring,' Macon said.

'There are worse things than boring, I've decided,' Sarah said. 'You know what I missed most when we were separated? The little things. Going to Eddie's for coffee on Saturdays. Waiting forever while you decided whether to buy a new screwdriver.'

He held her hand on the table, wrapping his fingers round hers. He knew the small, neat shape of it so well.

'For a while I was seeing another man, you know,' she said.

'Well, fine; whatever,' he told her.

'But it didn't work out,' Sarah said. 'After a certain age I think people just don't have a choice. You're who I'm with. It's too late for me to change. I've used up too much of my life now.'

In his mind Macon could hear Muriel asking, *You mean to tell me you can just use a person up and then move on?*

'*You're who I'm with. It's too late for me to change,*' Sarah said.

It seemed so, was the answer. Even if he had stayed with Muriel, he would then have left Sarah behind.

'After a certain age,' he told Sarah, 'it seems to me you can only choose what to lose.'

✧　　✧　　✧

While Sarah was at her art class, Macon worked on his Canada book, but his mind wasn't on the job. He stared out of the open window at a bush, where a bee was buzzing from flower to flower. Was it time for the bees already? Did Muriel know? Would she remember what a single bee could do to Alexander?

She was so careless, so unthinking; how could he have lived with someone like that? Her untidy habits, her misuse of words. There was no way she would remember about the bees.

He reached for the phone on his desk and dialed. 'Muriel?'

'What,' she said flatly.

'This is Macon.'

'Yes, I know.'

He paused. He said, 'Um, it's bee season, Muriel. I mean summer comes along so quickly, and I was just wondering if you'd thought about Alexander's injection.'

'Don't you believe I can manage that myself?' she shouted.

'Oh. Well.'

'You think I'm that stupid I can't remember even the simplest thing? So useless I can't even take care of my own son?'

'Well, I wasn't sure, you see, that—'

'A fine one you are! You desert that child without a goodbye and then you call me up to tell me I'm not a good mother!'

'No, wait, Muriel—'

'Dominick is dead,' she said.

'What? Dominick? The boy who fixes your car?'

'Not that you would care. It was his night to take my car and coming home he crashed into a guardrail. Died at once.'

'Oh, my God.' Macon rested his head in his hand.

'I have to go now and sit with his mother,' Muriel said.

'Is there something I can do? Stay with Alexander, maybe?'

'Alexander's got people of our own to stay with him,' she said.

The doorbell rang, and Edward started barking.

'Well, I'll say goodbye now,' Muriel said. 'Sounds like you have company. I'll let you get back to your *life*.' She hung up.

It was the men delivering the new couch. Macon showed them where to put it, and after they had gone, he sat down on it, still wrapped in its plastic covering. He rubbed his hands on his knees. Edward barked in the kitchen. Macon went on sitting.

When Ethan died, Macon had to go and look at the body. Sarah had waited outside. But later, and in the weeks that followed, she had demanded to know what he had seen, what he had felt, if in fact it had been Ethan at all lying there.

Remembering those conversations now, he began to believe that people could in fact be used up – could use each other up, could be of no further help to each other and maybe even do harm to each other. Maybe, he thought, who you are when you're with somebody matters more than whether you love her.

God knows how long he sat there.

Edward had been barking in the kitchen all this time, but now he began to bark even more loudly. Somebody must have knocked. Macon rose and went to the front door, where he found Julian. 'Oh. It's you,' Macon said.

'Thought I'd bring you the information for Paris,' Julian said.

Macon led the way to the living room. 'Just a few details to get right on the Canada guide,' he said, 'and then . . .'

Julian didn't seem to be listening. He sat down on the plastic-covered couch, and put his papers on the floor.

'Do you think Rose is not coming back?'

Macon hadn't expected him to be so direct. 'Oh, well, you know how it is,' he said. 'She's worried about the boys. They're living on tinned soup or something all the time.'

'Those are not boys, Macon. They're men in their forties.'

Macon rubbed his chin.

'I'm afraid she's left me,' Julian said.

'Oh, now, you can't be sure of that.'

'I care about that sister of yours more than anything in the world,' Julian said. 'And our marriage was working out fine. But that house of hers has become a kind of habit or something, and she just can't break free of it. It's like she can't help herself.'

Macon said, 'Why don't you give her a job, Julian?'

'Job?'

'Show her your office. The untidiness, that filing system you never get organized, that secretary who can't remember any appointments. Don't you think Rose could put all that right?'

'Well, sure, but—'

'Call her up and tell her your business is going to pieces. Ask if she could just come in and get things organized, get things under control. Use those words. *Get things under control*, tell her. Then sit back and wait.'

Julian thought that over.

'You're right,' he said. 'You're absolutely right.'

❖   ❖   ❖

Sarah came home at five-thirty. She found Macon standing in the kitchen with a cup of coffee. They went to inspect the new couch together, and practiced pulling it out to turn it into a bed. It made Macon think of Muriel's house, reminding him of all the times Muriel's sister had slept over on the couch in the living room.

They had been invited by some neighbors for supper, and as

they were getting dressed, Sarah said, 'Macon, you never asked me if I slept with anyone while we were separated.'

Macon paused, halfway into his shirt.

'Don't you want to know?' she asked him.

'No.' He put on the shirt and buttoned it up.

'The trouble with you is, Macon—'

It was shocking, the violent rush of anger he felt. 'Sarah, don't even start. By God, that kind of thing is just what's wrong with being married. "The trouble with you is—" and "I know you better than you know yourself—"'

'The trouble with you is,' she continued, 'you think people should stay in their own closed boxes. You don't believe in opening up, in sharing feelings, give and take.'

'I certainly don't,' Macon said, putting on his tie.

'You know what you remind me of? That telegram Harpo Marx sent his brothers: *No message. Harpo.*'

Macon laughed. Sarah said, 'You *would* think it was funny.'

'Well? Isn't it?'

'It isn't at all! It's sad! Getting a telegram like that would make me wild with anger!'

✧   ✧   ✧

After the supper he and Sarah walked home. The teenagers who had to be home by eleven o'clock were just returning, jumping out of cars shouting, 'See you! Thanks! Call me tomorrow!'

Later in bed, with Sarah breathing softly beside him, Macon heard the older kids coming home for twelve o'clock, and after that there would be the one o'clock group, laughter and car doors shutting and porch lights going out all along the street. In the end, he would be the only one left awake.

12

Paris

The plane to New York was a little bird of a thing, but the plane to Paris was huge, more like a building. Inside, great crowds were taking off their coats, pushing bags under seats. Babies were crying, mothers were speaking sharply to children.

Macon took his seat and was joined by an old couple speaking French. They nodded to Macon, but did not smile. He looked up at the passengers still coming in. A Japanese man carrying several cameras, a young girl in a sun hat. A woman in a white suit, with a little red case, her hair a dark tent, her face a thin triangle.

Muriel.

First he had that warm feeling you get when you recognize a face among strangers. And then: *Oh, my God*, he thought.

When she passed him, she looked at him and he saw that she'd known he was there. 'I'm going to France,' she told him.

'But you can't!' he said.

The French couple looked at him curiously. More passengers arrived behind Muriel, and she had to move on.

Sarah would find out about this, Macon thought. Somehow she would know. She had always said he had no feelings and this would prove it – that he could say goodbye so lovingly and then fly off to Paris with Muriel. Well, it was none of his doing and he wasn't going to take the blame.

When the plane was in the air, he tried to study Julian's notes, but he could not concentrate. A few hours later he got out his shaving things and went to the back of the plane. Unfortunately, there was a line of people and he had to wait. He felt someone arrive at his side. He looked and there was Muriel.

He said, 'Muriel, what *are you doing*? You can't afford the fare. And anyway, how did you know which flight I was on?'

'I called your travel agent. I borrowed from Bernice and a bit from my sister. And I'm going to Paris!'

'But why, Muriel? Why are you doing this?'

She lifted her pointed little chin. 'Because I felt like it.'

'You felt like spending five days alone in a Paris hotel?'

'You need to have me around,' she said. 'You were falling to pieces before you had me.'

A door opened and a man came out of one of the toilets. Macon stepped inside and locked the door behind him. He wished he could disappear, or at least go back and undo all the untidy, unthinking things he'd been responsible for in his life.

If she had read even one of his guidebooks, she'd have known not to travel in white.

When he came out, she had gone. For the rest of the flight he did not go near the back of the plane, and on arrival in Paris he hurried through the airport, and into a taxi to his hotel. It was one of those old Parisian hotels where mechanical things often went wrong. One of the two elevators was out of order and the phone in his room did not work. He unpacked, then went to the window and looked out over the rooftops.

How would she manage alone in such an unknown city?

He thought of how she was at home, knowing everything and everybody, wise and clever in the ways of her neighborhood. But she didn't know Paris. She might not have any money, she did not speak a word of the language . . .

By the time he heard her knock, he was so anxious that he almost ran to open the door.

'Your room is bigger than mine is,' she said. She walked to the window. 'I have a better view, though. Just think, we're really in Paris! Want to go to Chez Billy for breakfast? That's what your guidebook recommends.'

'No, I don't. I can't,' he said. 'You'd better leave, Muriel.'

'Oh. Okay,' she said. She left.

Sometimes she did that. She would push till he felt trapped, then suddenly pull back. You were so unprepared that you fell flat on the ground, Macon thought. You felt so empty.

He decided to phone Sarah. It seemed important to get in touch with her, although it was still night-time at home. He had to go down to the telephone in the hotel lobby.

Sarah sounded confused and sleepy. 'Who is that?'

'Sarah, it's Macon. I'm sorry I woke you but I wanted to hear your voice. How's the weather there at home?'

'The weather? I don't know. I don't think it's light yet.'

'I wish I was there. We could do some gardening today.'

'But you hate gardening! Macon, are you all right?'

Yes, he was fine, he told her. He'd had a good flight over, and yes, maybe he was a bit tired.

✧　　✧　　✧

Fried eggs, baked eggs, ham omelets, plain omelets. All day he walked blindly through the streets, writing notes in his guidebook. He did not go near Chez Billy. In the evening he returned to his hotel, leg muscles aching, and fell onto his bed. Two minutes later he heard a knock.

'Look,' Muriel said, coming in with her arms full of clothes. 'Just look at what I bought.' She held up for Macon's inspection a red evening dress, coats and jackets and trousers.

'Have you gone crazy?' Macon asked. 'What did all this cost?'

'Almost nothing!' she said. 'I found a place that's like the granddaddy of all thrift shops. This French girl I met at breakfast told me about it. I said how nice her hat was and she told me where she got it. And I found my way there, using your book!'

'But how will you get it all on the plane?'

'Oh, I'll find a way. Now, I'll take all this back to my room so we can go eat.'

Macon stiffened. He said, 'No, I can't.'

'What harm would it do to eat supper with me, Macon? I'm just someone from home you happened to meet in Paris!'

When she put it that way, it seemed so simple.

They went to the Burger King on the Champs-Elysées. Macon wanted to recheck the place anyway.

'Who's looking after Alexander?' he asked her.

'Oh, different people.'

'What different people? It can really upset a child that age—'

'Don't worry, he's fine. Claire has him in the daytime and then Bernice comes in and cooks supper and any time Claire is going out with the General the twins will keep him or if the twins can't do it then the General says Alexander can . . .'

Singleton Street rose up in front of Macon's eyes, all its color and confusion.

After supper they returned to their hotel, and in the elevator Muriel asked, 'Can I come to your room for a while?'

The elevator stopped at his floor. 'Muriel,' he said. 'I've been married to her forever. Longer than you've been alive, almost. I can't change now. Don't you see?'

She just stood in her corner of the elevator, looking young and sad and lonely.

'Goodnight,' he said.

He got out, and the elevator door slid shut.

✧   ✧   ✧

Large hotels, small hotels, hotels with old dirty wallpaper, modern hotels with huge American beds. Outdoor cafés, bar prices, restaurant signs, fixed-price menus . . .

In the early evening Macon headed wearily back to his own hotel. In the street ahead of him he saw Muriel. Her arms were full of parcels, her hair was flying out, her high-heeled shoes were tapping quickly along. 'Muriel!' he called, and ran after her.

'Oh, Macon, I've had the nicest day,' she said. 'I met these people from Dijon and we had lunch and they told me . . .'

He helped carry her parcels up to her room and sat down to watch her trying on all her new clothes.

'So, where are we having dinner tonight?' she asked.

'Well, I guess it's time to try someplace special.'

'Oh, goody!'

They went to a little restaurant in a side street, and Muriel began to study the menu. 'Just order Salade Niçoise,' Macon told her. 'It's always safe. I've been all through France eating that.'

'Well, that sounds kind of boring,' Muriel said.

She asked the waiter's advice, and he directed her toward a fresh tomato soup and a special kind of fish. Macon decided to have the soup too.

'Where are you going tomorrow, Macon?' she said.

'Out of Paris. Tomorrow I start on the other cities.'

'Take me with you.'

'I can't.'

At the end of the evening she said she was having bad dreams and would he come to her room to guard against them. He said no and told her goodnight. And then he felt how she drew at him, pulling deep strings from inside him.

In the night he thought of a plan to take her with him. What harm would it do? It was only a day trip. In the morning he picked up the phone to call her, but he had forgotten to report that it was out of order. He bent down behind the bed to see if he could fix it himself.

And his back went out.

No doubt about it. He had done it before and he recognized the signs. The pain was so sharp that he caught his breath. Very slowly and carefully, he lowered himself to the bed and lay there, wondering what to do next. He rearranged his travel plans in his mind. If he canceled one trip, changed another . . . Yes, he could do it in two days, as long as his back was better by tomorrow.

He heard a knock, and a voice. 'Macon? You in there?'

He did not answer. Somehow the pain in his back had cleared his head, and he saw how dangerously close he had come to falling in with her again. What luck his back had stopped him.

Later in the morning he got himself down to the hotel lobby and phoned Julian's office. A woman's voice answered, one that he thought he recognized.

'Rose? Is that you? What are *you* doing there?'

'Oh, Macon. Yes, I work here now. I'm putting things in order. You wouldn't believe how disorganized this office is.'

'Rose, my back has gone out on me.'

'Oh, no! Are you still in Paris?'

'Yes, but I need to change the plans for my day trips and . . .'

'I'll take care of everything,' Rose said. 'Just leave it with me. Get back to bed and rest your back.'

❖   ❖   ❖

The hotel waiter brought him food, and the chambermaid helped him to the bathroom. They were very kind and seemed quite anxious about him. Macon thanked them over and over.

The next day he heard a knock on the door and thought it was Muriel, but a key turned in the lock and in walked Sarah.

She wore a neat little suit and had two matching cases, and an air of efficiency and problem-solving about her.

'Now everything's taken care of,' she told him. She kissed his forehead, and brought him a glass of water. 'I'm going to make your day trips for you. I'll start tomorrow. And here are some painkiller pills I got from your doctor. Take one now.'

'But how did you get here so soon?' he asked.

'Thank Rose for that,' she said. 'She's turned Julian's office on its head and it now runs like a machine. Now, you go to sleep, and I'll go and get things organized.'

He slept, woke, slept again. Sarah brought him another pill.

'Sarah, those pills are deadly. My mind feels all foggy.'

'They help control the pain, don't they?'

He sighed, and took the pill. She sat down on the edge of the bed, careful not to cause any movement to his back.

'Macon,' she said quietly. 'I saw that woman friend of yours.'

His muscles tightened, and his back screamed at him.

'She saw me, too,' Sarah said. 'She seemed very surprised.'

'Sarah, she came over on her own. I promise you! She followed me. I didn't know till just before the plane took off. I told her I didn't want her along. I told her it was no use.'

She kept looking at him. 'You didn't know till just before the plane took off,' she said.

'Yes,' he said. 'It's true. You must believe me.'

'I believe you,' she said.

He spent the afternoon in another heavy, drugged sleep, and in the evening woke to find Sarah had brought in a supper of cold meats and fruit.

He sat up in bed, being careful of his back.

'This is very nice, Sarah,' he said.

'I was thinking,' Sarah said, 'that after I've done the day trips, if your back is better, we could have a little vacation. Take some time for ourselves, since we're here.'

'Fine,' he said. 'Great idea.'

He watched her put out their supper on flattened paper bags. 'Your plane ticket is for tomorrow morning, so we'll change that

'She saw me, too,' Sarah said. 'She seemed very surprised.'

for a later date,' she said. 'I left my ticket open-ended. Julian said I should. Did I tell you where Julian is living now? He's moved in with Rose and your brothers.'

'He's what?'

'I took Edward over to Rose's to stay while I was gone, and there was Julian. He sleeps in Rose's bedroom; he plays cards with them all every night after supper.'

'Good God!' Macon said.

'Have some of this cold meat.'

He accepted a slice, changing position as little as possible. As they ate, Sarah talked about their neighbors at home, about her art class, and how her teacher was pleased with her work.

'Good for you,' Macon said.

Sarah passed him a piece of fruit.

'Macon,' she said. 'Just tell me this. Was her little boy the reason you stayed with her?'

'No, it wasn't. Look, it's over. Can't we leave it now? I don't question you endlessly, do I?'

'But I don't have someone following me to Paris!' she said.

'And what if you did? It wouldn't be your fault.'

'You saw her before the plane left the ground. You could have told her to get off, that you never wanted to see her again.'

'You think I own the airline, Sarah?' Macon said.

'You could have taken steps to stop her,' Sarah said. 'If you'd really wanted to.'

And then she rose and cleared away their supper.

Later, she gave him his next pill, but he hid it in his hand and did not take it. He lay with his eyes closed, listening to Sarah getting ready for bed. She fell asleep almost at once.

How often had he taken steps in his life? Never. His marriage, his two jobs, his time with Muriel, his return to Sarah – all these had simply happened to him. He couldn't think of a single important act that he had done himself.

Was it too late now to begin?

Was there any way he could learn to do things differently?

He opened his hand and let the pill fall among the bedclothes. He would not sleep now, but anything was better than that heavy, drugged feeling.

In the morning, he got cautiously out of bed, and moving slowly and carefully got shaved and dressed. He packed his overnight bag. Then Sarah woke and sat up in bed.

'Macon? What are you doing?'

'Sweetheart, I'm packing to leave, and to catch my plane.'

'You're going back to that woman,' she said.

'Yes, I am,' he said. 'I thought about it most of last night. It's not the easy way out, believe me.'

She sat staring at him. She wore no expression. 'Macon? Are you just trying to get even with me for the time I left you?'

'No, sweetheart.' He closed his overnight bag.

She got out of bed. 'I suppose you realize what your life is going to be like. You'll be one of those couples no one invites to parties. They'll say, "My God, whatever does he see in her?" And her friends will no doubt ask the same about you.'

'That's probably true,' Macon said. Yes, he thought, that's how such couples happen. They come together for reasons that the rest of the world would never guess.

'I'm sorry, Sarah. I didn't want to decide this,' he said.

He put his arm around her painfully, and after a pause she let her head rest against his shoulder.

✧   ✧   ✧

Out in the street he could not see any taxis so he began to walk. Walking was quite easy but carrying his bag did terrible things to his back. Did he really need it, actually? His passport and plane ticket were in his pocket . . . He put the bag down by a shop wall and walked on. At last he saw a taxi and managed to stop it.

He got in, and told the driver where he was going. The taxi made a U-turn, and Macon realized he had been walking in the wrong direction. He sat carefully, trying to protect his back from bumps in the road.

The taxi stopped at some lights, and he watched a fair-haired boy in the street, whose walk reminded him of the way Ethan used to walk. And for the first time the memory did not feel like an icy hand closing round his heart. Maybe he was beginning slowly to accept these memories, that they were part of him, and that he could live with them.

The taxi went past Macon's hotel, and there outside stood Muriel, waving wildly at passing taxis, surrounded by suitcases and shopping bags and boxes full of red material.

'*Arrêtez*!' Macon cried to his driver, and the taxi braked sharply. A sudden flash of sunlight caught the taxi window, and little jewels seemed to fly across the glass. They were probably old water spots, but for a moment Macon thought they were something else. They were so bright and joyful, for a moment he thought they were wedding confetti.

GLOSSARY

allergy (*adj* **allergic**)   a medical condition that causes people to react badly or feel ill after eating (or breathing) something

basement   a room or rooms below the level of the ground

bee   a black and yellow flying insect that stings, and makes honey

cluck (*v & n*)   to make a short low sound with your tongue against the roof of your mouth

comfort (*n*)   something that helps you when you are suffering, worried, or unhappy

confetti   small pieces of coloured paper thrown over a married couple in celebration at a wedding

crutches   two long sticks that you put under the arms to help you walk after you have injured your leg or foot

exhaust tube   a pipe carrying air or gas coming out of a machine

faucet (*American*)   a device that controls the flow of water from a pipe (*British English* **tap**)

frizzy   (of hair) very tightly curled

Goddammit   a swear word, used to show anger or annoyance

groceries   food of all kinds, sold in shops and supermarkets

growl (*v*)   to make a low sound in the throat, as a sign of anger

honey   a word you use for somebody you like or love

howl (*n & v*)   a long loud cry, showing pain or anger

hug (*v*)   to put your arms round somebody and hold them

injection   putting medicine or drugs into the body with a syringe

Jesus (**Christ**)   a swear word, used to show surprise

joyful   very happy; causing people to be happy

lean (*v*)   to bend or move from an upright position

leash   a long piece of leather or rope, used for controlling a dog

limp *(v)* to walk with difficulty because one leg is injured

Martian an imaginary person (creature) from the planet Mars

moan *(n)* a long deep sound, expressing suffering or unhappiness

nervous anxious or afraid

pantry a small room in a house, used for storing food

plaster (**cast**) a white plaster case that covers a broken bone

porch a small area at the entrance to a house, covered by a roof

praise *(n & v)* words that show approval or admiration

ridiculous very silly or unreasonable

rug a piece of thick material like a small carpet

rump the part of an animal's body at the top of its back legs

scared frightened or afraid

screwdriver a tool with a narrow blade, used for turning screws

sigh *(n)* letting out a long breath, to show you are tired, sad, etc.

sink *(n)* a fixed container in a kitchen, with a piped water supply

stroke *(v)* to move your hand gently over something

system (*adj* **systematic**) an organized set of ideas or a particular way of doing something

Thanksgiving a public holiday in the US (the fourth Thursday in November), when a traditional meal is eaten

thrift shop *(American)* a shop that sells inexpensive, second-hand clothes and other things

turkey a large bird, similar to a chicken, but bigger

twins two children born at the same time to the same mother

veterinary hospital (**vet's**) a place for treating or looking after animals who are sick or injured

wearily showing tiredness; without interest or enthusiasm

ACTIVITIES

Before Reading

1 **Read the story introduction on the first page of the book, and the back cover. Then match these names to the sentences below.**

Macon / Sarah / Rose / Ethan / Charles and Porter / Edward / Julian / Muriel

1 She is not married, and lives with two of her brothers.
2 He is causing problems because he bites people.
3 She has left her husband and wants to divorce him.
4 They are divorced from their wives and live with their sister.
5 He employs people to write guidebooks for Americans who are traveling on business.
6 Her job is to teach dogs to behave properly.
7 He dislikes traveling but writes tourist guides for a living.
8 He dies before the story begins.

2 **What do you think Macon will do in the story? Choose some of these ideas.**

Macon will . . .

1 divorce his wife.
2 get back with his wife.
3 fall in love with somebody else.
4 get rid of Edward.
5 be bitten by Edward.
6 live with his sister and brothers for the rest of his life.
7 begin to write a different kind of guidebook.
8 move to Paris to live.

While Reading

Read Chapters 1 and 2. Then match each person to their description. What else have you learned about them so far?

Rose / Edward / Muriel / Julian / Sarah

1 _____ was once bright and sociable, but now is nervous and unhappy.

2 _____ is very concerned about her brothers and their families, but also sees them clearly for what they are.

3 _____ is very small, with short legs, and is starting to get out of control.

4 _____ is loud and cheerful, and wants to get on with things.

5 _____ is thin, talkative, and friendly – maybe too friendly.

Before you read Chapter 3, think about the three women – Rose, Sarah and Muriel – and then answer these questions.

1 What would each woman do if Macon asked her for help?

2 Which woman will Macon actually ask for help, and why do you think he will choose this one?

Read Chapters 3 to 5. Think about what has happened to these relationships in these chapters. Which people are now closer together, and which are further apart?

1 Macon and Sarah

2 Macon and Muriel

3 Rose and Julian

4 Rose and her brothers

Before you read Chapter 6, can you guess what Macon will do about Muriel's invitation?

1 He will make an excuse and not go. (Does he write, phone, visit, or ask another person to tell her?)
2 He will go, but leave early after an uncomfortable evening.
3 He will take Muriel and Alexander out for a meal instead.
4 He will go round to the house to make an excuse, but end up staying there.
5 He will go to dinner with Muriel and enjoy himself.
6 He will pretend to forget about the invitation, and not answer the phone when Muriel calls.

Read Chapters 6 to 9. Who are Macon and Muriel talking to? What are they talking or thinking about? What do these things tell us about Macon and Muriel, and about their relationships with other people?

Macon:

1 'I don't have friends anymore and everyone looks silly and foolish and not related to me.'
2 'You want to marry Rose?'
3 'If he just watches, he won't learn how to do it.'
4 Macon held those cool little fingers in his, and felt a pleasant kind of sadness running through him. Oh, danger had returned to his life. He was forced to worry once again about wars and disasters and the future of the world.

Muriel:

5 'Aren't you going to ask how Alexander is?'
6 'I expect you want to stop seeing me.'
7 'You're seventeen years old and you can do what you like.'

Before you read Chapter 10, what advice would you give to Macon now? You can change or add to the reasons if you want.

1 Stay with Muriel – you have a new life now.
2 Go back to Sarah – she knows you better than anybody.
3 Go back to living with your brothers – they've been through divorces and they can help you.
4 Go back to living on your own – it's too soon for a serious relationship with any woman.

Read Chapters 10 and 11. Some characters find it hard to change ways of thinking or behaving from their past. What habits or ways of thinking are suggested by these remarks?

1 Macon to Muriel: 'I don't think people should get married.'
2 Muriel to Macon: 'You wouldn't ever leave me, would you?'
3 Rose to Macon: 'I kept losing that apartment, somehow.'
4 Macon to Muriel: 'I was just wondering if you'd thought about Alexander's injection.'
5 Sarah to Macon: 'The trouble with you is, Macon—'

Before you read Chapter 12, what do you think will happen at the end of the story? Choose some of these ideas.

1 Macon will stay with Sarah.
2 Macon will go back to Muriel.
3 Rose and Julian will separate and then get divorced.
4 Julian will move into Rose's house with Rose and her brothers.
5 Julian will begin a relationship with Sarah.
6 Sarah and Muriel will become friends.
7 Macon will decide to live alone.
8 Macon will move to San Francisco and become a keen traveler.

After Reading

1 **Maybe this is what some of the characters in the story are thinking. Which characters are they, and what has just happened in the story at that moment?**

1 'Well, thanks, Ma. You really know how to make me look good, don't you? Why do you do it? He's probably already thinking about leaving me. Just like everybody else. All thanks to you.'

2 'Maybe if I eat some turkey, it'll show her that I *am* falling in love with her. I don't care if it makes me ill. I think she's wonderful. I don't know why her family are so mean to her about her cooking.'

3 'She's shouting at Macon again. It's because of whatever was in that big envelope the mailman just brought. I hate it when she shouts. I'm going to get a drink, then keep out of the way.'

4 'I'll have to say something, tell him how worried we all are. His house is a mess, and he doesn't even *care!* I just don't understand him. This awful woman . . . Why is he ruining his life for her?'

5 'When I saw him today, it was like old times. And I'm sure he felt that too, the way he looked at me. Am I fooling myself? Maybe, but . . . *they* don't look like a couple to me. And *we* do.'

6 'Just a day trip. We can easily get there and back in a day. She can look at the shops while I check the hotels. That can't do any harm, can it? Yes, I'll call her right away . . .'

2 Here are four people talking about either Macon or Muriel.
Complete each passage by choosing one suitable word to fill each
gap. Then choose the right label to go with each passage.

Claire talking to her mother about Macon
Alexander talking to Claire about Macon
Charles talking to Rose about Muriel
Julian talking to Rose about Muriel

1 'She's just not the right woman _____ him. She's not even
pretty, and _____ clothes are awful. And you should _____
her house! It's so untidy, and _____ just walk in and out when
_____ like. And she doesn't speak proper _____ either. I just
do not understand _____ he is ruining his life for _____.'

2 'He's okay. I didn't like him _____ he first came. He kept trying
_____ teach me things and make me _____ things. But then he
brought Edward, _____ is wonderful! And he stops Mom _____
about me so much – I can _____ all kinds of food now.'

3 'I've met her at last! She's _____ lively – always doing things,
talking to _____. I think she's just what Macon _____. He's
more relaxed around her; he's _____ so worried about all his
little _____ working properly. She wears strange clothes,
_____ somehow they suit her. It's as _____ he's not an
accidental tourist in _____ own life any more.'

4 'Leave him alone! He's a nice _____, but you might scare him
away _____ you're not careful. He's got a _____ job, he's
fantastic at fixing things _____ the house, and he makes
Muriel _____. Okay, he hasn't got divorced yet, _____ so what?
The two of them _____ work things out in their own _____.'

3 Choose adjectives and phrases (as many as you like) from the list to say what each of these quotes tells us about Macon. What changes (if any) do you see in Macon by the end of the story?

afraid of being hurt / avoids getting involved / boring / cautious / concerned for other people / kind / logical / practical / selfish / sensible / sympathetic / thoughtful / thoughtless / unadventurous / unfeeling / unsympathetic / unwilling to take risks

1 'If you don't see any point to life, I can't see why a rainstorm would make you nervous.'

2 ROSE: 'You should have asked her in.'
   MACON: 'I was afraid she'd say no.'

3 'All I'm saying is I want Alexander to learn to add up!'

4 'Call her [Rose] up and tell her your business is going to pieces. Ask if she could just come in and get things organized, get things under control . . . Then sit back and wait.'

5 'Just order Salade Niçoise. It's always safe. I've been all through France eating that.'

4 Here are Macon's and Sarah's views of their relationship. Which ideas do you find the most convincing, and why?

MACON: He began to believe that people could in fact be used up – could use each other up, could be of no further help to each other and maybe even do harm to each other. Maybe, he thought, who you are when you're with somebody matters more than whether you love her.

SARAH: 'After a certain age I think people just don't have a choice. You're who I'm with. It's too late for me to change. I've used up too much of my life now.'

5 Sarah knows about Macon's relationship with Muriel because Rose tells her. Complete Rose's side of their conversation.

SARAH: You said you had something to tell me, Rose. What is it?
ROSE: _____

SARAH: Another woman? Oh. Who is she? How did he meet her?
ROSE: _____

SARAH: Yes, Macon mentioned those lessons. What's she like?
ROSE: _____

SARAH: And what do Charles and Porter think of her?
ROSE: _____

SARAH: In other words, none of you likes her. Is it serious, this relationship? How often does Macon see her?
ROSE: _____

SARAH: *Living* with her? I see. And what's this 'something else' I ought to know?
ROSE: _____

SARAH: A little boy? Oh my God.

6 What did you think of this story? Think about these questions and how you would answer them, and write a short report of the story.

1 What, for you, were the saddest and funniest moments in the story?

2 If you were on a long plane flight, which character from the story would you most like to sit next to, and which would you least like to sit next to? Explain why you think this.

3 Did Macon choose the right woman in the end? Do you think they are likely to stay together? Why, or why not?

4 How did you find the ending? Did you feel it was sad, hopeful, satisfying, unexpected, disappointing? Describe your reaction.

ABOUT THE AUTHOR

Anne Tyler was born in Minneapolis in 1941. She grew up in North Carolina, but has lived in Baltimore, Maryland, for most of her adult life. She married an Iranian physician in 1963, and was widowed in 1997. She has two daughters, both of whom have done illustrations for her books.

Her novels tend to have three things in common: Baltimore settings, life events (marriage, death, losing a job), and everyday characters. They are about 'ordinary families with extraordinary problems', but always focus on family life rather than on global or historical events. Some critics have described Tyler as a modern-day Jane Austen, because of her perceptive observation of relationships and life's daily difficulties.

Tyler has said that she thinks of her work 'as a whole' – as a 'town full of lots of people I've made up'. Asked if her characters ever surprise her, she answered, 'All the time.' She begins a novel by making a short outline, but she doesn't always follow it. 'I always think I know how they'll end, but I'm almost always wrong. In the case of *The Accidental Tourist*, I actually began a chapter in which Macon stayed with Sarah. But it didn't work; something in the characters themselves persuaded me the ending would have to be different.'

Anne Tyler has written nearly twenty novels. *Breathing Lessons* won the Pulitzer Prize in 1989, and *The Accidental Tourist* (1985) won the National Book Critics Circle Award. Four of her novels have been filmed, including *The Accidental Tourist*. In the 1988 film of the novel William Hurt played Macon, and Geena Davis won an Oscar for her performance as Muriel.

OXFORD BOOKWORMS LIBRARY

Classics • Crime & Mystery • Factfiles • Fantasy & Horror
Human Interest • Playscripts • Thriller & Adventure
True Stories • World Stories

The OXFORD BOOKWORMS LIBRARY provides enjoyable reading in English, with a wide range of classic and modern fiction, non-fiction, and plays. It includes original and adapted texts in seven carefully graded language stages, which take learners from beginner to advanced level. An overview is given on the next pages.

All Stage 1 titles are available as audio recordings, as well as over eighty other titles from Starter to Stage 6. All Starters and many titles at Stages 1 to 4 are specially recommended for younger learners. Every Bookworm is illustrated, and Starters and Factfiles have full-colour illustrations.

The OXFORD BOOKWORMS LIBRARY also offers extensive support. Each book contains an introduction to the story, notes about the author, a glossary, and activities. Additional resources include tests and worksheets, and answers for these and for the activities in the books. There is advice on running a class library, using audio recordings, and the many ways of using Oxford Bookworms in reading programmes. Resource materials are available on the website <www.oup.com/bookworms>.

The *Oxford Bookworms Collection* is a series for advanced learners. It consists of volumes of short stories by well-known authors, both classic and modern. Texts are not abridged or adapted in any way, but carefully selected to be accessible to the advanced student.

You can find details and a full list of titles in the *Oxford Bookworms Library Catalogue* and *Oxford English Language Teaching Catalogues*, and on the website <www.oup.com/bookworms>.

STARTER • 250 HEADWORDS

present simple – present continuous – imperative –
can/cannot, must – *going to* (future) – simple gerunds …

Her phone is ringing – but where is it?

Sally gets out of bed and looks in her bag. No phone. She looks under the bed. No phone. Then she looks behind the door. There is her phone. Sally picks up her phone and answers it. *Sally's Phone*

STAGE 1 • 400 HEADWORDS

… past simple – coordination with *and*, *but*, *or* –
subordination with *before, after, when, because, so* …

I knew him in Persia. He was a famous builder and I worked with him there. For a time I was his friend, but not for long. When he came to Paris, I came after him – I wanted to watch him. He was a very clever, very dangerous man. *The Phantom of the Opera*

STAGE 2 • 700 HEADWORDS

… present perfect – *will* (future) – *(don't) have to, must not, could* –
comparison of adjectives – simple *if* clauses – past continuous –
tag questions – *ask/tell* + infinitive …

While I was writing these words in my diary, I decided what to do. I must try to escape. I shall try to get down the wall outside. The window is high above the ground, but I have to try. I shall take some of the gold with me – if I escape, perhaps it will be helpful later. *Dracula*

... *should, may* – present perfect continuous – *used to* – past perfect –
causative – relative clauses – indirect statements ...

Of course, it was most important that no one should see
Colin, Mary, or Dickon entering the secret garden. So Colin
gave orders to the gardeners that they must all keep away
from that part of the garden in future. *The Secret Garden*

STAGE 4 • 1400 HEADWORDS

... past perfect continuous – passive (simple forms) –
would conditional clauses – indirect questions –
relatives with *where/when* – gerunds after prepositions/phrases ...

I was glad. Now Hyde could not show his face to the world
again. If he did, every honest man in London would be proud
to report him to the police. *Dr Jekyll and Mr Hyde*

STAGE 5 • 1800 HEADWORDS

... future continuous – future perfect –
passive (modals, continuous forms) –
would have conditional clauses – modals + perfect infinitive ...

If he had spoken Estella's name, I would have hit him. I was so
angry with him, and so depressed about my future, that I could
not eat the breakfast. Instead I went straight to the old house.
Great Expectations

STAGE 6 • 2500 HEADWORDS

... passive (infinitives, gerunds) – advanced modal meanings –
clauses of concession, condition

When I stepped up to the piano, I was confident. It was as if I
knew that the prodigy side of me really did exist. And when I
started to play, I was so caught up in how lovely I looked that
I didn't worry how I would sound. *The Joy Luck Club*